UNIQUE
Colorado

A Guide to the State's Quirks, Charisma, and Character

Sarah Lovett

John Muir Publications
Santa Fe, New Mexico

Special thanks to Abbie and Bob Casias; Rich Grant and Jean Anderson, Denver Metro Convention & Visitors Bureau; Margaret Walsh, Colorado History Museum; Donna Lepik, Colorado State Fair; Dave Steinke, U.S. Forest Service; Dave Roberts, Pueblo Levee Mural Project; Tom Aver, *Bloomsbury Review;* Brad Rhea, Living Tree Project, Sterling.

John Muir Publications, P.O. Box 613, Santa Fe, New Mexico 87504

First edition. First printing July 1993.

Library of Congress Cataloging-in-Publication Data
Unique Colorado : a guide to the state's quirks, charisma, and character / Sarah Lovett. — 1st ed.
   p. cm.
  Includes index.
  ISBN 1-56261-103-8 : $10.95
  1. Colorado—Guidebooks. 2. Colorado—Miscellanea. I. Title.
F774.3.L67 1993
917.8804'33—dc20   93-13452
                                               CIP

Design and Typography: Ken Wilson
Illustrations: Bette Brodsky
Typeface: Belwe, Oz Handicraft
Printer: Malloy Lithographing

Distributed to the book trade by
W. W. Norton & Co.
New York, New York

Cover photo © Leo de Wys Inc./Rick Rusing
Cover photo inset © Leo de Wys Inc./Steve Vidler
Back cover photo, Snowboarding at Vail © Jack Affleck

CONTENTS

INTRODUCTION

Denver Metro Convention & Visitors Bureau

Wildflowers bloom in front of the majestic Front Range

Nothing but Rocky Mountains, skiers, vistas, and more vistas—that's Colorado, right? Ride the lift to the top of Aspen Mountain, or picnic on top of Pikes Peak, and no one would argue that you're in the Centennial State. Of course, there are many things still to discover about unique Colorado. For instance, did you know that Colorado has two national grasslands, four state wildlife refuges, 12 national forests, 25 designated wilderness areas, 40 state parks, and 222 state wildlife areas? Did you ever imagine that Colorado hosts some of the world's most official burro races? Or did you know that there are festivals to celebrate mountain men and women, ticks, and calf-roping hot-air balloonists? Have you ever tried a recipe for sweet and sour elk meatballs? And have you ever wondered just how much gold was extracted from them thar' hills?

Unique Colorado presents key facts, intriguing destinations, handy charts, quick-access maps, and entertaining trivia in a user-friendly format. Where else can you find a recipe for Anasazi wild rabbit stew, a map of historic forts, the best location for ice climbing, a guide to gold mines and ghost towns, tips on the best recreational spots, literary locations, and a rating system for microbrewery beers?

Festivals abound in the Centennial State

You can open to any page and find readable, entertaining, unusual information bites. The index will guide you to specific topics and sites. The table of contents is designed to give you an idea of what subjects each section covers. However you choose to use this book, you'll soon discover what is unique about Colorado. ❧

The Rocky Mountain bighorn sheep is Colorado's state animal

COLORADO

Population:
3,372,558

Area:
104,651 sq. miles

Capital: Denver

Nickname:
Centennial State or Silver State

Date of Statehood:
August 1, 1876

Highest Elevation:
Mt. Elbert 14,433 ft.

State Flower:
Columbine

State Bird:
Lark bunting

State Motto:
Nil Sine Numine
(Nothing Without Providence)

THEN AND NOW

In the Beginning

Dinosaurs Rule

One-hundred-and-forty-five million years ago, dinosaurs ruled the northwest corner of Colorado, the area now protected as **Dinosaur National Monument**. Stegosaurus, Apatosaurus (commonly known as Brontosaurus), and Diplodocus browsed among ferns, cycads, and tall conifers; flesh-eating Allosaurus preyed on these great vegetarians.

For millions of years the dinosaurs lived and died, and river waters collected their carcasses on a sandbar. A shallow sea covered much of Colorado at the end of the dinosaur age and the animals' bones were preserved under layers of sediment deposited by the tides. Finally, dissolved silica permeated the layers, the river bed became sandstone, and the bones were mineralized. As the Rockies to the east were created by geologic action, the dinosaur remains were exposed.

Between 1908 (when paleontologist Earl Douglass began his search for fossils) and 1924, 350 tons of dinosaur bones and their case rock were excavated in the area that is now Dinosaur National Monument. Dinosaur bones can only be seen at **Dinosaur Quarry**.

FYI: Park Headquarters, Hwy. 40, 2 miles east of Dinosaur; 303-374-2216. To reach the quarry, enter the park near Jensen, Utah, and take the shuttle bus from the parking lot; 801-789-2115.

FYI: The **Denver Museum of Natural History**, 2001 Colorado Blvd.; 303-322-7009.

FYI: **Dinosaur Valley**, 362 Main St., Grand Junction (there's a paleontological laboratory here and constantly updated research); 303-243-DINO; or 303-242-0971 if you're interested in working on an actual dig through the **Museum of Western Colorado**.

FYI: Visit **Rabbit Valley Dinosaur Quarry** (hike past unexcavated dinosaur bones and working digs) 24 miles west of Grand Junction, off I-70. 🦕

A float down the **Green** or **Yampa** rivers might be the best way to experience Dinosaur National Monument. The tradition dates back to 1825 when General William H. Ashley (a Missouri pelt trader) rode the rapids of Lodore Canyon. Famed explorer-scientist John Wesley Powell covered the same route in 1869. These days, there are numerous reputable outfitters and a wide variety of trips to choose from. *FYI:* Write to the Superintendent, Dinosaur National Monument, P.O. Box 210, Dinosaur, CO 81610; 303-374-2216.

Florissant Fossil Beds National Monument

In Colorado 35 million years ago, sequoias, palm trees, hickories, tsetse flies, birds, butterflies, and giant katydids thrived in a subtropical climate. Care to take a trip back in time? The fossils of these plants and animals have been preserved in the Eocene epoch rocks of Lake Florissant, which was formed between 38 and 26 million years ago when volcanic activity dammed several streams. Continued sporadic volcanic action for the next half a million years trapped countless species of plants and animals and covered the lake with dust, ash, and pumice. Eventually, plant and animal remains in the lake bed became fossilized as ash turned to sedimentary rock. *FYI:* Half a mile from Florissant on Teller County Rd. No.1; P.O. Box 185, Florissant, CO 80816.

Mesa Verde is one of the foremost Anasazi sites in the U.S.

300 B.C.–A.D. 1500

A Day in the Prehistoric Life

If you think your day is tough, imagine an average day in the life of the Anasazi people who inhabited what is now **Mesa Verde National Park** and other areas of the Southwest for more than 700 years.

On a typical summer day, A.D. 1100, your a.m. might be spent in the courtyard sharpening stone and bone tools—knives, axes, scrapers, awls—or crafting bowls, ladles, canteens, jars, mugs, and other pottery goods. There was breakfast to be made, perhaps a corn porridge heated by hot rocks placed inside clay pots or pitch-lined baskets. Crops of corn, beans, and squash had to be tended, while nuts, seeds, and other wild edibles needed to be gathered. Dogs and turkeys were domesticated, but killing squirrels, rabbits, and deer demanded energetic effort by hunting parties. If you had a minute to spare, there were hunting nets and sandals to weave out of yucca fiber, and rabbit-hide robes and turkey-feather blankets to mend for winter wear. At days end, men might retreat to the kiva, while women finished decorating the latest batch of black-on-black ceremonial clay ware. The evening called for a bit of story-telling by elders to lull the kids to sleep. If you were safely bedded down in your six-by-eight-foot stone room when you remembered you'd forgotten to take the garbage out, never fear. The Anasazi lobbed their food scraps and broken tools and wares over the nearest cliff; in that respect, they were very much like us.

Mesa Verde National Park is one of the foremost Anasazi sites in the U.S. **Chapin Mesa** and **Wetherill Mesa** are the location of major cliff dwellings. The park is heavily visited; you might want to plan your visit in late fall or early spring. *FYI:* Superintendent, Mesa Verde National Park, CO 81330; 303-529-4465 or 303-529-4475. 🔔

Crow Canyon Archaeological Center is a not-for-profit organization committed to high quality archaeological research and education. Work with professionals in the field or in workshops. Fees charged help support Crow Canyon research. *FYI:* 23390 County Rd. K, Cortez 81321; 800-422-8975 or 303-565-8975.

Prehistoric Trivia Quiz

1) In Mesa Verde's classic times, A.D.1100 to 1300, related family groups probably lived together as a clan that was _____. Each clan may have had its own kiva and agricultural land-use areas.
  a) patrilineal (descent traced through the male ancestors)
  b) matrilineal (descent traced through female ancestors)
2) Indiana Jones would have no trouble keeping busy in Colorado. There are more than _____ known prehistoric sites in the state, and they all contain treasure of the archaeological sort.
  a) 15,000 **b)** 25,000 **c)** 75,000
3) Peabody Museum archaeologist Noel Morss spent several years in east-central Utah where he determined **Fremont Culture** to have had some horticultural skills, a somewhat sedentary lifestyle, and the use of _____. Colorado Uinta Fremont sites have been excavated in Dinosaur National Monument.
  a) written language **b)** metal **c)** ceramics

ANSWERS: 1) b 2) b 3) c

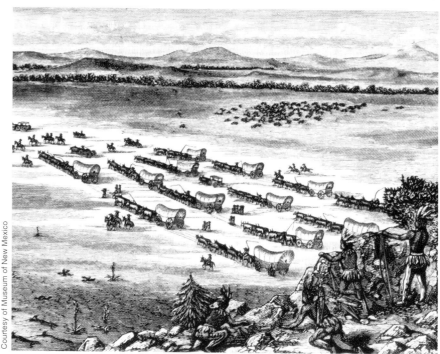

Courtesy of Museum of New Mexico

An ox-train on the Santa Fe Trail

1540–1850s

Pathfinders Timeline

1540: Spanish expansionist Francisco Vasquez de Coronado journeyed north from Mexico in search of riches and the fabled "seven cities of Cibola." Instead of golden streets, he encountered resistance from the Pueblo Indians, but his quest opened up the Southwest to Spanish settlement.

1776: Fray Francisco Atanasio Dominguez and Fray Sylvestre Velez de Escalante, with a small group of soldiers, left Santa Fe, New Mexico, on a six-month journey in search of a northern route to the recently established California missions. The Frays explored much of Utah and southwestern Colorado.

1803: The Louisiana Purchase doubled the area of the United States. Zebulon Pike led the first U.S. expedition into Colorado territory by way of the Arkansas River in 1806. Pike (a New Jersey boy) and 16 soldiers set out from St. Louis in June dressed in summer clothes, confidently expecting an October return. In November, they were still wandering around the Colorado plains when they spotted "Pikes Peak." Although Pike was eventually captured by the Spanish, he managed to explore much of southern Colorado.

1820: Major Stephen H. Long guided the expedition which explored the Front Range of the Rockies—the area Long called the "Great American Desert." After Long, fur traders and trappers swarmed into Colorado as the demand for beaver headgear became the rage in the East and on the Continent. Jedediah Smith, Jim Beckwourth, Jim Bridger, and Kit Carson were among the pelt dealers.

1821: Mexico gained its independence from Spain and the **Santa Fe Trail** officially opened to foreign trade. William and Charles Bent and Ceran St. Vrain constructed Bent's Fort—which served as a major pit stop for twenty years—on the Mountain Branch of the Santa Fe Trail. Today, Highways 50 and 350 retrace roughly 188 miles of the **Mountain Branch**—from the Arkansas River crossing at the Kansas border through the Comanche National Grassland to Raton Pass and the New Mexico border. 🐾

History Trivia Quiz

1) Although no permanent Spanish settlement was established in Colorado until 1852 in the San Luis Valley, the Spanish gave the state its name; "Colorado" means _____.
   a) canyon **b)** ruddy or reddish
   c) land of color

2) Fashion trends come and go like lightning, and beaver hats were no exception. Western entrepreneurs were quick to fill the beaver void with _____ skins. Within decades, the once-plentiful animal was almost extinct, and Plains Indians saw the end of their way of life.
   a) snake **b)** rabbit **c)** buffalo

3) 1846 was a headline year for the Santa Fe Trail; merchandise valued at ____ passed through Colorado.
   a) more than $1 million
   b) $600,000 **c)** $200,000

ANSWERS: 1) b 2) c 3) a

1840s–1860s

Wars and Gold

In 1846 an expansion-hungry United States went to war with Mexico. Two years later, Mexico ceded its land in the American Southwest to U.S. victors in the Treaty of Guadalupe Hidalgo. The new territory was fair game for anyone desperate or daring enough.

An old-timer pans for gold

Colo. Historical Society

Glorified tales of the discovery of gold at Cherry Creek launched the **Pikes Peak** gold rush of 1859—and Colorado's wildest, liveliest, most colorful period. Fortune seekers arrived by wagon, on horseback, even on foot, pushing their meager possessions in wheelbarrows. By the early 1860s, gamblers, working women, Eastern establishment college grads, and con artists had joined the miners in Front Range towns like Breckenridge, Georgetown, and Fairplay. *FYI:* You can (and probably should) hike Pikes Peak. Most folks use **Barr Trail**, which runs about 13 miles each way. Begin off Ruston Ave. by the cog railway station.

After much debate and the proposal of various names—Yampa, San Juan Colorado, and even Lula (for a miner's sweetie)—Colorado was officially established as a territory in 1861.

Pikes Peak Trivia

☞ Some of the best competitors in the country vie for the gold at Pikes Peak or Bust Rodeo held each August at Colorado Springs Penrose Stadium.

☞ Mario Andretti, Al and Bobby Unser, and Roger Mears have all won America's second oldest auto race, Race to the Clouds. Course contestants climb Pikes Peak each July.

☞ At Pikes Peak summit, view Denver 70 miles to the north, the Sangre de Cristo Mountains and the Spanish Peaks to the south, and the Mosquito and Sawatch ranges due west.

☞ Pikes, a "14er" topping 14,110 ft. elevation, is America's best known peak.

☞ Bill Williams (a Texan, of course) used his nose to propel a peanut to the top of Pikes Peak in 1929. It only took twenty days!

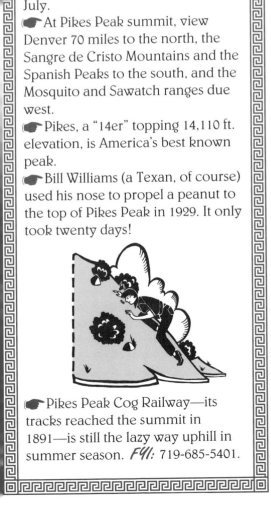

☞ Pikes Peak Cog Railway—its tracks reached the summit in 1891—is still the lazy way uphill in summer season. *FYI:* 719-685-5401.

William Gilpin (1815–1894)

William Gilpin served as a major in the Mexican War and fought Comanches on the Santa Fe Trail before heading home to Independence, Missouri, to practice law, wheel and deal, and oppose slavery. He also became one of the West's most eloquent champions. Although Gilpin was a dreamer, he was also a politician. Ignoring death threats, he cast the single vote for Abraham Lincoln in Independence in 1860, and he began an astute and successful campaign for the position of governor of the Colorado Territory.

Gilpin was concerned about the lack of military protection should approaching Rebel forces decide to go for the gold. He organized the 1,342-member First Regiment of Colorado Volunteers, "Gilpin's Lambs." These barely trained clerks, actors, mule skinners, con men, lawyers, bartenders, and preachers suffered casualties at the Battle of Glorieta Pass, March 28, 1862, but they managed to turn back General Sibley's Confederate forces.

1850s–1880s

Treaties and Trouble

The gold rush signaled trouble for the Cheyenne and Arapahoe as Anglo travelers overran grazing and hunting grounds and introduced new diseases to native peoples. An 1851 Senate treaty declared that nine Plains tribes were to receive 50,000 dollars' worth of trade goods for each of fifty years in exchange for development rights—including army installations and roads—within the Indian nations. Ten years later—when U.S. Government abuses of the treaty were painfully clear—the Indian Bureau convinced four chiefs to sign a new treaty at Fort Wise. They exchanged Cheyenne-Arapahoe lands of 1851 for 5 million arid acres between the Arkansas River and Sand Creek. The tribes were ordered to farm 40-acre plots and to give up buffalo hunting, the basis of their subsistence. Hostilities between Anglos and Indians increased, with atrocities committed by both sides, until 900 mounted soldiers under the command of Colonel John A. Chivington attacked the teepee village of Cheyenne chief Black Kettle on November 29, 1864. The one-sided slaughter continued for ten hours. Eight soldiers and perhaps 200 Cheyenne, many of them women and children, were left dead. *FYI:* Today, there is a small plaque marking the massacre site, on County Road 96 outside Lamar. The site is on private property. ॐ

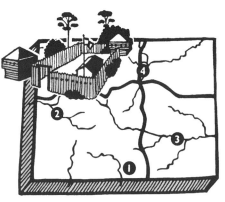

Forts

Colorado Forts

Nothing remains of the military posts named Crawford, St. Vrain, Sedgewick, Misery, and Wicked—perhaps abandonment had something to do with their names. But the following provide a glimpse of the past.

1) Fort Garland: Built in 1858—and named for Brigadier General John Garland—this fort was abandoned in 1883. It functioned as trade center and protection for settlers. The restored fort is now a museum run by the Colorado Historical Society. *FYI:* 719-379-3512.

2) Fort Uncompahgre: French trapper Antoine Roubidoux established this trading post in 1826. Wood and sod huts form the perimeter. Each year an encampment is open to the public. *FYI:* 303-874-8349.

3) Bent's Fort: Started by the Bent brothers in 1831 as a trading post, it also served as a rest stop for travelers on the Mountain Branch of the Santa Fe Trail. Fully restored. *FYI:* 719-384-2596.

4) Fort Vasquez: This was a thriving trading post for Indians, trappers, and hunters. Louis Vasquez built the fort in 1835-36. A WPA replica stands today. *FYI:* 303-785-2832.

Chief Ouray (c. 1820–1880) and Chipeta (White Singing Bird) (c. 1843–1924)

The six bands of Colorado Utes (related linguistically to Aztecs) were isolated and spared some of the problems that threatened the Plains tribes. Although the Utes did not have the martial reputation of the Cheyenne, Comanches, and Kiowas, they were formidable enemies. For awhile, Utes and Anglos formed an uneasy alliance against the Cheyenne, and Ute Chief Ouray negotiated treaties with the U.S. government. Chipeta (White Singing Bird), Ouray's wife, also worked hard to keep peace between whites and Native Americans, but Ute territory was reduced acre by acre. When Indian agent Nathan Meeker was killed by a band of northern Utes in 1879, the tribe was relocated to Utah and a small reservation in southwestern Colorado.

1876–1900

In a State

By chance, America was celebrating its 100th year when President Grant declared Colorado the Union's 38th state on August 1, 1876. From then on, Colorado was commonly known as the "Centennial State." In the proposed constitution, white and black males had the right to vote, but the Constitutional Convention voted 24 to 8 to deny women of any color suffrage. The newly organized Colorado Women's Suffrage Association had done its best to earn Colorado the honor of being the first state in the Union to acknowledge suffrage as a human right and extend the vote to females. The all-male convention no doubt feared female inclusion in "man's domain" and also thought the innovation would hurt the territory's chances for statehood. Wyoming was the first state to grant full female suffrage. *FYI:* The gold-domed **Colorado State Capitol** in Denver, 1475 Sherman St., is a favorite stop for visitors; 303-866-2604. 🔔

Nothing extended the course of development and Manifest Destiny like the great Iron Snake. In 1870 the Denver Pacific Spur connected Denver to Cheyenne, Wyoming, and the Union Pacific's Transcontinental Line. Before long, the Denver and Rio Grande Railroad crossed the state, and the narrow gauge opened up remote mining towns to profitable commerce. On November 1, 1887 the first steam locomotive chugged into Aspen and local cows were so aghast they stopped producing milk for days. Today, Colorado's narrow

Colo. Historical Society

The railroad spurred Manifest Destiny

Narrow Gauge Railroads

gauges are the best in the world. (Note: These trains run on a seasonal basis; call before planning your trip.)

1) Black Hawk and Central City: The train is pulled by famed Engine No. 71 during the 30-minute ride from Central City. You'll see the "Richest Square Mile on Earth."

2) Cripple Creek and Victor: Debark from Cripple Creek Depot for a 4-mile, 45-minute trip by coal-burning steam locomotive. *FYI:* 719-689-2640.

3) Cumbres and Toltec: The longest and the highest narrow gauge railway starts in Chama, New Mexico, and ends in Antonito, Colorado. It's a day trip of tunnels, gorges, and mountains. *FYI:* 719-376-5483.

4) Durango & Silverton: More than 200,000 people take the train each season. Start in Durango and follow the same route as prospectors and gamblers did a century ago—a 46-mile trip and 2,768-foot climb to Silverton. *FYI:* 303-247-2733.

5) Georgetown Loop Railroad: The famous Loop turns 14 stomach-churning curves. The train ascends 3 miles in 2 1/2 circles and crosses the Devil's Gate Bridge. *FYI:* 303-569-2403.

Silver Lining
The late 1860s brought the demand for more efficient and sophisticated methods of ore extraction and processing. Nathaniel Hill resolved the problem of ore reduction in 1868 when he opened his Boston and Colorado Smelter in the town of Black Hawk. "Boom" was the key word in the 1870s and 1880s, and silver outclassed gold as the ore of the decade.

Modern Times

If you're one of the three million people living in Colorado today, you enjoy a standard of living that's higher than the national average, an unemployment rate that's going down, not up, and the nation's lowest death rate. Like citizens of other southwestern states, Coloradoans tend to cluster in several heavily settled areas. Denver's population is dense (there are more than 4,500 people per square mile), and five Colorado counties have more than 200 people per square mile. In contrast, nine of the Centennial State's counties have less than four people per square mile.

While Colorado's economy is a blend of high-tech industries, light manufacturing, transportation, ranching, and agriculture, the biggest boom is the tourist and recreation industry. Twenty million visitors flock to the state each year. ໃ▲

The **Ute Mountain Reservation** covers half a million acres in the southwest corner of the state. Towaoc, at the base of Sleeping Ute Mountain, is the site of reservation headquarters. Anasazi ruins, recreation areas, and the Ute Mountain pottery plant are located on the reservation. *FYI:* 303-565-3751.

Colo. Historical Society

Ute Indians

Patricia Shroeder (b. 1940)

Patricia Shroeder was born in Portland, Oregon, but moved to Colorado in 1960s. She has been a Democratic U.S. Representative for the First District in Colorado since 1973.

Modern Trivia Quiz

1) Construction on the **Royal Gorge Bridge** was completed in ____.

a) 1929 **b)** 1643 **c)** 1256

2) In 1934, gold bullion valued at more than _____ was shipped from San Francisco to the **Denver Mint**. This is the third largest gold storehouse in the nation. Tours are popular. Keep your eyes open for machine gun turrets that date back to the 1929 market crash. *FYI:* W. Colfax Ave. and Cherokee St.; 303-844-3582.

a) $150 million **b)** $3 billion **c)** $1 billion

3) In 1979, Nancy Dick became the first Colorado woman to become _____.

a) Chief of Police **b)** an astronaut **c)** Lieutenant Governor

4) Clear air, _____, and high altitude have contributed to the selection of Colorado as a pilot training area. Facilities built during WWII are still important—especially the **Air Force Academy** in Colorado Springs. This is the third most popular tourist stop in the state. The setting is spectacular and the 17-spire Cadet Chapel is an architectural coup. *FYI:* 719-472-1818.

a) good weather **b)** money **c)** friendly people

5) Deep inside Cheyenne Mountain, the **North American Aerospace Defense Command** is a city on springs behind 25-foot-thick doors. NORAD has been built to survive _____. If you want to take a tour in six months, book now. *FYI:* NORAD Public Affairs, 3SSW/PAC, Attn: Tour Program, Peterson AFB, CO 80914-5000; 719-554-7895.

a) Godzilla and Mothra **b)** UFOs **c)** nuclear attack

ANSWERS: 1) a 2) b 3) c 4) a 5) c

THE NATURAL WORLD

Pilot Peak from Beartooth Highway

Roller coaster variations in elevation, a full range of geologic formations, and a legion of life zones contribute to the complexity of Colorado's ecology, geology, and topography. Plains, mountains and plateaus—each accounting for roughly a third of the state's acreage—are the topographic divisions in Colorado.

Rocky Going

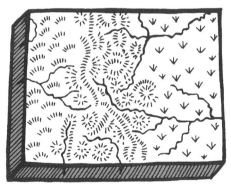

 Mesas

 Mountains

Meadows

Colorado is situated on the North American Plate, which was once attached to Europe and a part of Gondwanaland, the mega-continent. Roughly 300 million years ago, plate activity cracked the earth's crust north to south through Colorado, which resulted in the creation of the first Rocky Mountains. These Rockies eroded for 200 million years or so and then, about 60 million years ago, uplift began to form the second Rocky Mountains. They took shape around the same time North America and Europe parted company (which in turn created the Atlantic Ocean).

A recent uplift (about 5 million years ago) may also be due to plate motion. This uplift of the Colorado Plateau resulted in the division of the plateau into basins. Between uplifts, volcanoes rocked what is now Colorado and created the San Juan Mountains. Later eruptions occurred in the Golden area, the San Luis Valley, and the Rabbit Ears Range and Spanish Peaks. For 3 million years, while the Pleistocene gave Colorado the big chill, glaciers carved and scoured the earth. The end of the Pleistocene marked the beginning of human endeavors in Colorado—at least that's what the latest finds indicate.

Peak Experience

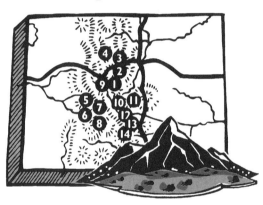

14ers

Colorado's mountain peaks may be the state's most astounding feature, and like Cyrano's nose, you can't miss them. At least 53 peaks are higher than 14,000 feet (hence the nickname "the 14ers"), while more than a thousand mountains are at least 2 miles high. Most peaks—the Rockies, for instance—are part of a north-south alignment; the east-west Uintas are the exception. Colorado's highest peak, Mt. Elbert (14,433 feet), is guaranteed to make the toughest hiker huff and puff. **North Mt. Elbert Trail** (4.5 miles to the summit) is heavily traveled. Pick up the trailhead at Halfmoon Campground (via Halfmoon Creek Rd., which is also Forest Rd.110). **South Mt. Elbert Trail** is longer (about 6 miles to summit) and less traveled. Lake View Campground (close to Twin Lakes) is the trailhead.

1. Mt. Sherman, 14,036'
2. Mt. Democrat, 14,148'
3. Quandary Peak, 14,265'
4. Mt. of the Holy Cross, 14,005'
5. Capitol Peak, 14,130'
6. Maroon Peak, 14,156'
7. Pyramid Peak, 14,018'
8. Castle Peak, 14,265'
9. Mt. Elbert, 14,433'
10. Huron Peak, 14,005'
11. Mt. Oxford, 14,153'
12. Mt. Harvard, 14,420'
13. Mt. Princeton, 14,197'
14. Mt. Shavanno, 14,229'

Keith L. Grove /USDA Forest Service

Slater Falls

Go With the Flow

Colorado marks the beginning of four of the West's mega-river systems: the Arkansas, Colorado, Platte, and Rio Grande. Prehistoric and modern human migration routes were guided by Colorado's major drainages. The state has more than 8,000 miles of streams and over 2,000 lakes. FYI: Division of Wildlife, Central Regional Office, 6060 Broadway, Denver 80216; 303-297-1192.

1) Animas: *Las ánimas* is Spanish for "the spirits" or "the souls." Lots of fish have been pulled from these waters, but there seem to be plenty more, including record-length brown trout. Good fishing on public waters south of Durango to the Southern Ute Indian Reservation.

2) Arkansas: Its headwaters flow from the Mosquito Range near South Park, then the river courses east across southern Colorado and eventually empties into the Mississippi River.

3) Big Thompson: This river grows strong in Rocky Mountain National Park and

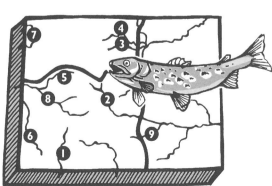

Rivers

flows through Big Thompson Canyon before reaching the plains. Good fishing below Grandpa's Retreat near Estes Park (no bait). Brook, rainbow, and brown trout.

4) Cache la Poudre: (a.k.a. just plain Poudre) Long stretches of this river parallel Hwy. 14 toward Fort Collins. Brown and rainbow trout (average length 11 inches), also fighting whitefish. Fly fishing here, some lures and worms, and eggs. Two wild trout sections—no bait allowed (near Fort Collins and Rustic).

5) Colorado: After being joined by the Fraser River, this is Gold Medal water, but almost all the river is private. Incidentally, the Colorado River might very well have been the Grand River (Utah's preference) but for the wiliness of Colorado politicians. The state legislature renamed the river in 1921—when the Utah legislature was out of session and not available to protest.

6) Dolores: This one joins the Colorado near Moab, Utah. Frays Escalante and Dominguez explored the hauntingly beautiful canyons in 1776. These days, the pro-McPhee Dam folks enjoy the great rainbow, brown, and cutthroat trout which thrive in the tame waters. Catch and release designation for the 12 miles between the dam and Bradfield Bridge.

7) Green: Peaceful until it turns south into the Gates of Lodore in Dinosaur National Monument and cuts through 17-mile Lodore Canyon; fasten your seat belt and follow the historical wake of Major John Wesley Powell.

8) Gunnison: Flows from the Elk Ranges and merges at Grand Junction with the Colorado River. Class IV and V rapids challenge expert kayakers along the 12-mile Black Canyon of the Lower Gunnison. Below the rapids, floating (for all levels) is the best way to watch red-tailed hawks, great horned owls and other raptors. A proposed dam may change this soon.

9) Huerfano: Headwaters are at Lilly Lake, above 14,000 feet in the Sangre de Cristos—used for irrigation throughout Herfano County. Camping and fishing; worms and salmon eggs recommended.

10) North Platte: With headwaters in North Park, the river drains into Wyoming and links with the South Platte in Nebraska. This is a Gold Medal stream where North Park browns are prominent. Use spinners, bait, and flies.

11) Purgatoire: By legend, this "river of lost souls" is said to gain its name from the Spanish explorers who died in its waters without benefit of the last rites of the church.

12) Rio Grande: It becomes a major New Mexico and Texas drainage eventually reaching the Gulf of Mexico. June is the month for wild raft races between Creede and South Fork. *FYI:* Creede/Mineral County Chamber of Commerce; 719-658-2374.

13) South Platte: It begins in South Park and flows to the northeast, growing more powerful from the Big Thompson, Cache la Poudre, and other tributaries. Both the north and south fork of this river offer good fishing.

14) San Juan: The river runs west through the Four Corners region and meets the Colorado at Glen Canyon. Rumor has it there are lunkers to be had below Pagosa Springs. Downstream of Navajo Reservoir, you need a New Mexico fishing license if you plan to cast; barbless flies and artificial lures here only—keep just one trout over 20 inches.

USDA Forest Service

This beaver makes it home in the Rio Grande

15) San Miguel: The rare metal Vanadium (discovered by Marie Curie), used for hardening steel, was mined in this river's canyons. Brown and rainbow trout are common, and the Royal Wulff is the preferred fly.

16) Uncompahgre: Its famous Ouray hot springs soothed Ute Indians. Today, you can soak your weary bones.

17) Yampa: The wild waters through Cross Mountain Gorge are death to kayakers and rafters. Deerlodge Park (Dinosaur National Monument) is a more rational launch point for rafters. You'll get a light roller coaster ride before joining the Green River at Echo Park. ❧

Ogden Tweto (b. 1912)

Geologist Ogden Tweto is "Mr. Colorado" to his colleagues, a title he earned because of his unsurpassed knowledge of the region. Tweto was born in North Dakota and spent much of his youth in Montana, where he developed an interest in geology. He received his bachelor's and master's degrees in geology from the University of Montana in 1934 and 1937, and earned his Ph.D. from the University of Michigan in 1947.

In 1940, he gained a full-time appointment with the U.S. Geological Survey; much of his 40-year-plus career has focused on Colorado's geology. Tweto compiled a new geologic map of Colorado in the early 1970s. It is generally agreed among geologists to be the finest such map in existence.

R.B. Taylor, USGS

Life in the Wild

The great highs and lows that mark Colorado's topography account for much of the state's living diversity. Plants and animals that have adapted to life at an elevation of 3,386 feet may find the going rough on the summit of Colorado's highest mountain, Mt. Elbert (elevation 14,433 feet). Each species or variety has its own requirements for continued survival, its own habitat or ecosystem.

The eastern plains are covered with short-grass prairie including wheat grasses, blue grama, blue stem, and buffalo grass. These plains may once have been tall-grass prairie but overgrazing—even back in the days of the bison—has cut them short. Cottonwood, willows, and shrubs thrive along rivers, while pricklypear and yucca flourish almost everywhere on the plains.

The mountains and plateaus support ponderosa pines, Douglas fir, spruce fir, piñon, juniper, shrubs, and tundra, which is found above 11,000 or 12,000 feet. Saltbrush, greasewood, and sagebrush grow on the semi-desert basins of the west.

A great way to see some of Colorado's plant and animal life is on your own two feet. *FYI:* On hiking and backpacking in national forests, contact the U.S. Forest Service, P.O. Box 25127, 11177 W. 8th Ave., Lakewood 80225; 303-236-9431.

The Wild Life

Prehistoric hunters depended on a fairly steady diet of bison, rabbit, mule deer, mountain sheep, elk, antelope, and fowl for survival. Today, Colorado's wildlife population includes coyote, mule deer, grizzly bears, nocturnal and diurnal raptors, marmots, bighorn sheep, blue grouse, mountain lions, pronghorn antelope, and prairie chicken. Unfortunately, Colorado has its share of threatened or endangered species. *FYI:* For a booklet on endangered wildlife, write to the Division of Wildlife, Colorado Department of Natural Resources, 6060 Broadway, Cenver, CO 80216-1000; 303-297-1192.

Endangered Animals

The animals below—only some of Colorado's jeopardized wildlife species—are judged by the state and the federal government to be threatened or endangered.

Grizzly bear   Endangered, Colo.;
                                    Threatened, Fed.
Gray wolf   Endangered, Colo. and Fed.
River otter   Endangered, Colo.
Lynx   Endangered, Colo.
Wolverine   Endangered, Colo.
Peregrine falcon   Endangered, Colo. and Fed.
Bald eagle   Endangered, Colo. and Fed.
Whooping crane   Endangered, Colo. and Fed.
Piping plover   Threatened, Colo. and Fed.
Greater sandhill crane   Endangered, Colo.
Greater prairie chicken   Endangered, Colo.
Wood frog   Threatened, Colo.
Humpback chub   Endangered, Colo. and Fed.
Bonytail   Endangered, Colo. and Fed.
Greenback cutthroat trout   Threatened, Colo. and Fed.

Colo. Historical Society

Getting around in Colorado is easier than it used to be

Access

Getting there can be all the fun. Colorado is traversed by 17 extremely scenic and historic highways, byways, and skyways. Look for the sign featuring a blue columbine. (Note: Most Scenic and Historic Byways are paved, but a few require four-wheel-drive vehicles.)

1) San Juan Skyway and the Million Dollar Highway: Getting to and from Colorado's mining towns was a real problem in the nineteenth century. Before 1880, for example, a freight load demanded three mule spans, two industrial strength wagons, and a skilled skinner. Ore transport cost as much as $80 a ton until Russian-born Otto Mears built his toll road to link Ouray with Ironton Park in 1883. Mear's stretch of road from Ouray to Ironton Park came to be known as the Million Dollar Highway—perhaps because gold-bearing gravels were used in its original grading, perhaps because the price tag was so high to adapt the road for motor vehicles, or perhaps because even a million dollars couldn't entice travelers to travel the road more than once. Today, the Million Dollar Highway is just a part of the 236-mile San Juan Skyway. Mountain vistas and old mining towns.

2) Mount Evans Byway: This 27-mile route from Idaho Springs to the summit of Mount Evans is the highest paved highway in North America. Great views of the Front Range of the Rockies.

3) The Flat Tops Trail: Connecting Meeker and Yampa, this 75-mile route traverses forests, canyons, and meadows. Spring wildflowers.

4) Pawnee Pioneer Trails: Cross the northeastern high plains between Sterling, Fort

Scenic and Historic Highways

Morgan, and Ault. Grasslands and the Pawnee Buttes are highlights of this 125-mile route. Sterling Reservoir.

5) The Highway of Legends: This 75-mile route links Trinidad, La Veta, and Walsenburg—the home country of many early Hispanic settlers.

6) The Gold Belt Tour: You'll need a four-wheeler for portions of this 122-mile route that follows the old Florence and Cripple Creek Railroad grade through Phantom Canyon. Views of Pikes Peak; access to the Garden Park Fossil Area.

7) The West Elk Loop: A 205-mile route between Carbondale, Hotchkiss, Gunnison, and Crested Butte. Alpine wildflowers; views from the north rim of the Black Canyon.

8) The Guanella Pass Byway: A 22-mile stretch between Georgetown and Grant; ghost mines, wildlife, and the view from the 11,669-foot pass.

9) Unaweep/Tabeguache Scenic and Historic Byway: Passing through Unaweep Canyon, Dolores River Canyon, and reaching the high plains of the Colorado Plateau, this 138-mile byway between Whitewater and Placerville is heaven for geologists.

10) The Peak-to-Peak Byway: Along these 55 miles between Estes Park and Black Hawk, you'll find remnants of the mining era.

11) Los Caminos Antiguos: A 96-mile byway between Fort Garland and Cumbres Pass through the San Luis Valley.

12) The Grand Mesa Byway: Start at Plateau River Canyon and continue 63-miles through meadows and forests to the top of Grand Mesa. Between I-70 and Cedaredge.

13) The Alpine Loop Byway: The 63-mile route links Lake City, Ouray, and Silverton. Top elevation is a mere 12,800 feet; four-wheel-drive required.

14) Silver Thread Byway: These 75 miles between South Fork and Lake City are filled with ghost towns and unusual geologic formations.

15) South Platte River Trail: A 14-mile route between Julesburg and Ovid; follow historic westward trails including the Pony Express Trail.

16) Cache la Poudre-North Park Byway: 101 miles of road through canyons, plains, over hogbacks and Cameron Pass. Connects Fort Collins and Walden.

17) Santa Fe Trail: Bent's Old Fort is located on this 188-mile byway. The Kansas state line near Holly and the New Mexico state line at Raton Pass are at opposite ends of this route that parallels the Mountain Branch of the Santa Fe Trail. 🐾

USDA Forest Service

Winter comes early in Colorado and stays late

Weathering the Weather

The Rocky Mountain climate has its own peculiarities, most noticeably the daily fluctuation between highs and lows—a 50-degree drop
at night is not unusual. There are four definite seasons in the Rockies.
Spring is noted for its wind and reversibility. Long after fruit trees
blossom, deep snows have been known to fall, and gusty days are the
norm. Summer brings warmer weather and thundershowers. July and
August are the hottest months, but nights are always cool. Fall is usually crisp and clear, but the occasional blizzard does blast its way
through the mountains. Aspens turn and the tourist crowds thin somewhat. Winter comes early (late October) and stays and stays (sometimes until early May). Bikinis and skis are unlikely (but not uncom-
mon) combinations in May and June. When winter blizzards strike,
they can definitely be ferocious, but they are seldom long-lived.

Denver Norms:

Month	J	F	M	A	M	J	J	A	S	O	N	D
Temperature	30	34	38	47	57	67	73	71	63	52	39	33
Precipitation	0.5	0.7	1.2	1.8	2.5	1.6	1.9	1.5	1.2	1.0	0.8	0.6

Grand Junction Norms:

Month	J	F	M	A	M	J	J	A	S	O	N	D
Temperature	26	34	42	52	62	72	79	76	67	55	40	28
Precipitation	0.6	0.5	0.8	0.7	0.8	0.4	0.5	0.9	0.7	0.9	0.6	0.6

Average Temperatures Statewide

season	high	low
winter	47	10
spring	69	27
summer	86	41
fall	75	3

Weather Trivia

Average annual number of sunny days in Denver: 296

Coldest day in Denver: February 8, 1936: -30 degrees

Hottest day in Denver: August 8, 1878: 105 degrees

Greatest Denver snowfall: December 1-6, 1913: 45.7 inches

Average annual rainfall in Denver: 15 inches

Average annual snowfall: 364 inches at Wolf Creek Pass; 140 inches at Aspen; 60.3 inches statewide

Worst flood: July 31, 1976, Big Thompson Canyon (near Estes Park): a flash flood drowned and crushed to death 160 people

Costliest hail storm: July 11, 1990, the most expensive hail storm in U.S. history resulted in 650 million dollars' worth in insurance claims

Coldest temperature: February 1, 1985, Maybell: -61 degrees

Greatest snowfall in 24 hours: (a record for the nation!) April 14-15, 1921, Silver Lake (20 miles west of Boulder): 76 inches

Highest wind speed: January 7, 1971, Boulder: 143 mph

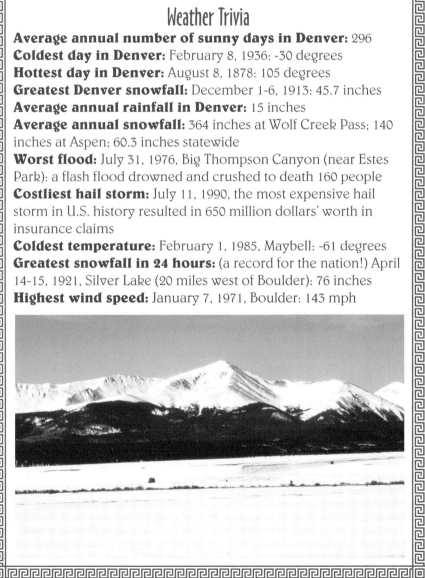

GOING TO TOWN

The gold-domed state capitol

Denver

Pop. 492,365
Elev. 5,280 feet
Noted for: Black American West Museum and Heritage Center; Denver Mint; Denver Center for Performing Arts; gold-domed capitol; Molly Brown House; more than 2,000 restaurants; multi-ethnic neighborhoods; Denver Broncos; golf; Cheesman Park; Denver Botanic Gardens; City Park; Cherry Creek State Recreation Area; Elitch Gardens Amusement Park
Nearby: Barr Lake State Park; Chatfield State Recreational Area; Red Rocks Park; Roxborough State Park; Golden Gate Canyon State Park; Mount Falcon Park; Waterton Canyon
Visitors' Information: 303-892-1112

Mile-high Denver sits on high rolling plains, just east of the Rockies

Boom and Bust

Prospector William Green Russell heard a rumor from his wife's Cherokee relatives that gold could be found in the Rockies. Returning from California, Russell organized a search party that eventually reached the mouth of Cherry Creek. Although Russell didn't strike a lode, his efforts inspired other gold-hungry prospectors to swarm into the area. By 1858 two small settlements—Auraria and Denver City—had sprung up on opposite banks of Cherry Creek.

In 1870, the Denver Pacific Railroad was completed after Governor John Evans, newspaperman John Byers, and Denverites raised $280,000 to finance the spur. Denver's population exploded in the next decade, and the city continued to fulfill the needs of both the mining and cattle industry.

The 1893 silver crash inspired the diversification and expansion of Denver's economic base. Parks, gardens, and tree-lined streets took the place of red light districts, and post-WWII brought another period of expansion. Denver hit the skids again in the mid-1980s when the world's oil glut led to a recession. Today, business in Denver has stabilized in a manner appropriate for a manufacturing and trade center. It's the largest city within a 600-mile radius, and it's ethnically diverse.

Denver Sports Trivia

☞ A major case of Broncomania packs 75,000 people into Mile High Stadium. Denver Bronco games are sold out years in advance.
☞ The Denver Zephyrs—the city's minor league baseball team—takes over Mile High Stadium each spring and summer.
☞ The Denver Nuggets pro basketball team dribbles like mad from November to May.
☞ You can surf or slide in summertime at Water World. *FYI:* 303-427-SURF.

Denver Festivals

Capitol Hill People's Fair - June
Cherry Blossom Festival - June
Colorado Renaissance Festival - June & July
Cinco de Mayo - May
Oktoberfest - October
Denver International Film Festival - October
National Western Stock Show and Rodeo - January

Leadville

Pop. 3,879
Elev. 10,152 ft.
Noted for: mountain biking on old mining roads (rentals available at 10th Mountain Sports); four-wheel-drive trips; 469 miles of hiking and cross-country skiing on the Colorado Trail; the National Mining Hall of Fame; Silver Dollar Saloon; Routes of the Silver Kings; the Leadville, Colorado & Southern Railroad
Nearby: Arkansas River; Sugar Loafin' Campground; Twin Lakes Area; Leadville Ski Country; Copper Mountain
Visitors' Information: 719-486-3900

Colo. Historical Society

Rich deposits of ore made Leadville the state's second largest city in its heydey

It's no wonder that Leadville was poppin' in 1880: almost $12 million in silver was pulled from area mines. Rich deposits of gold, silver, molybdenum, zinc, manganese, and turquoise have made Leadville one of the most mineralized areas in the world. In its heyday, Leadville was the second largest city in Colorado, boasting more than 25,000 inhabitants.

Leadville has gone by the name "Cloud City" because of its elevation and its situation above the timberline in the Arkansas Valley. To the west, beyond the Arkansas River, Mt. Massive (14,421 ft.) and Mt. Elbert (14,433 ft.)—two of Colorado's highest peaks—rise like giants. The Mosquitoes loom to the east. At their feet, the mineral rich Carbonate, Iron, and Fryer Hills have been stripped bare of trees.

H. A. W. Tabor (1830–1899) and Baby Doe McCourt (1854–1935)

Drawn by the Pikes Peak rush of 1859, Vermont-born H. A. W. Tabor traveled west with his remarkable wife, Augusta, and his son. They settled in Leadville where Tabor became mayor and postmaster and grub-staked a mine for two immigrant shoemakers. He became a rich man when the unlikely miners struck a 30-foot-thick silver vein known as the Little Pittsburg. Conned into purchasing a second, "worthless," mine, Tabor became a millionaire when his miners discovered the famous Chrysolite lode. Tabor's luck turned soon after he divorced his wife and married "Baby Doe" McCourt, a young divorcée. He died destitute in 1899, and Baby Doe kept vigil in a cabin next to the Matchless Mine for 36 years, until she froze to death.

Refining the Miners

Mining days were wild and the haves employed armed guards to protect themselves and their worldly goods from the have nots. While litigation overflowed court dockets and claim-jumpers battled squatters, Tabor built the **Tabor Opera House**. The other Carbonate Kings erected hotels, Victorian homes, and gas lights. In addition to the rich, gamblers, thugs, Harvard and Yale graduates, bull-whackers, and other opportunists kept the opera house in business. 🐎

Colo. Historical Society

Miners taking a break

Leadville Trivia

☛ Snow in July is no stranger to Leadville. In winter the ground freezes so deep it's been said that "gravediggers have to employ dynamite."

☛ During its most affluent years (1878-1880), Leadville's abandoned houses were torn town and used for firewood.

Leadville Festivals

Boom Days - August
Leadville Music Festival - July through early August
Oro City - late June through mid-July

Colo. Historical Society

Silverton nestles up against Anvil Mountain

Silverton

Pop. 794
Elev. 9,305 ft.
Noted for: marriages; ice skating; sledding; skiing; Hardrockers Holidays and Brass Band Festival each August; Teller House Hotel; Grand Imperial Hotel Barroom; San Juan County Historical Society Museum; Silverton Narrow Gauge; Old Hundred Gold Mine Tour—developed by bona fide miners, this tour includes a train ride to the center of Galena Mountain.
Nearby: excellent four-wheel-drive routes between Silverton—Lake City—Ouray—Telluride; San Juan Skyway; Million Dollar Highway; Alpine Loop; rugged Weminuche Wilderness; Purgatory-Durango Ski Resort
Visitors' Information: 303-387-5654

Snug in the lap of the San Juan Mountains, Silverton is the seat of rugged San Juan County, which boasts the highest mean elevation of any U.S. city. (Silverton also has the distinction of being the only community in San Juan County.)

Silverton was originally known as Baker's Park, named for Captain Charles Baker, the region's first recorded prospector. According to local lore, the town was re-dubbed Silverton when a mine operator reportedly remarked, "We may not have gold here, but we have silver by the ton." The land surrounding Silverton was acquired from Ute

Indians in 1873 through the Brunot Treaty. The narrow gauge Denver & Rio Grande Railway reached the town of Silverton on July 11, 1882. Silverton—in its entirety—was designated a National Historic Landmark by the Department of the Interior in 1966. Today, its personality is marked by the arrival of several **Durango & Silverton Narrow Gauge** trains each day. Annually, more than 200,000 tourists visit the town via narrow gauge. Stay longer than a few days and give yourself a chance to ease behind the scenes. You'll find the folks are friendly and the pace is more relaxed once the last train of the day pulls out of town.

Silverton Trivia

☛ If you need a breath of fresh air, Silverton may be just the place to inhale. According to ongoing government research, some of the purest air in the continental U.S. can be enjoyed on top of Molas Pass near Silverton.

☛ In Silverton, **weddings** are given special attention. Prospective couples can choose from a variety of settings, as well as between the county judge or a local minister. The narrow gauge train is a popular location. *FYI:* Silverton Chamber; 303-387-5654.

☛ The good guys and the bad guys shoot it out (well, pretend to) on main street each evening during the summer season.

☛ Silverton is under the watchful eye of the **Christ of the Mines Shrine** which stands on Anvil Mountain. When mining slumped in the 1950s, the Christ statue was carved in Carrara, Italy, shipped over, and the shrine completed. Soon after, Sunnyside Mine recommenced mining until 1991. *FYI:* By foot up 10th Street and by car on Shrine Road.

Colo. Historical Society

Downtown Ouray is now a National Historic District

Ouray

Pop. 684
Elev. 7,811 ft.
Noted for: Hot springs (Orvis, Ouray, Wiesbaden); four-wheel-drive trips; cross-country skiing; Ouray County Historical Museum (housing a collection of Victorian antiques); Bachelor-Syracuse Mine Tour (one hour long and one of the state's best); St. Elmo Hotel
Nearby: Million Dollar Highway; San Juan Skyway; Uncompahgre River and Gorge; Ridgway; Red Mountain Pass; Box Canyon Falls; big game hunting; ice climbing
Visitors' Information: 303-325-4746; 800-228-1876

Fourteenth-century Ute Indians were the first known residents of this area of the Rockies. They found plentiful game, rivers, and natural hot springs, as well as protection from the Plains Indians. By the mid-nineteenth century, gold and silver prospectors were arriving en masse. Early white residents named their first town in honor of the great Ute chief Ouray, who was responsible for averting bloodshed between the Utes and Anglos during the tribe's last days in western Colorado.

As mining continued, more than 10,000 tunnels and shafts were cut by hardrockers within a 10-mile radius of the town. These days, old miner's trails—like Corkscrew Road, Pough-keepsie Gulch, and Imogene, Engineer, and Black Bear Pass—attract those who crave four-wheeling thrills. Downtown Ouray is a National Historic District offering visitors the chance to view dozens of well-preserved Victorian structures.

Ouray Festivals
Culinary Art Show - September
Cabin Fever Days - President's Day weekend

Central City and Black Hawk

Pop. 329
Elev. 8,496 ft.
Noted for: limited stakes gambling; Central City-Black Hawk National Historic District; Central City Opera House; Teller House and Teller House Casino; Lace House; Gilpin House County Museum

Central City in the 1860s

Colo. Historical Society

Nearby: four-wheel-drive excursions; interesting cemeteries; Arapaho National Forest; Golden Gate Canyon State Park
Visitors' Information: 303-592-1502

John H. Gregory was among the lucky when he struck gold in 1859 in what was later known as Gregory's Gulch. His strike launched the state's first major gold rush. Side by side, the mining camps of Black Hawk and Central City grew up on either side of the gulch. Central City grew so quickly it challenged Denver as the center of Colorado civilization. Its tradition of theater and opera has lasted more than a century.

Black Hawk had its own stroke of luck when Nathaniel P. Hill built the Boston-Colorado Smelter in the town in 1867. The smelter gave the mining industry a needed boost by making it economically feasible to extract refractory gold ore.

Today, limited stakes poker, blackjack, and slots are adding a different flavor to these towns. In the Old West, there was no limit, but some folks don't relish the problems that legalized gambling may bring to Colorado's "New West."

Central City and Black Hawk Festivals

Lou Brunch Day - June
Summer Opera Festival - early July to mid-August
Central City Jazz Festival - August

The historic courthouse overlooks main street

T.R. Youngstrom

Telluride

Pop. 1,047 (2,400 Telluride area)
Elev. 8,800 ft.
Noted for: scenic beauty; four-wheel-drive routes; festivals; ski resort; mountain biking; fly fishing; golf; Telluride National Historic District; New Sheridan Hotel and Sheridan Bar
Nearby: Uncompahgre National Forest; San Juan Hut Systems; ghost towns; McPhee Recreation Area; Miramonte Reservoir; Ridgway State Recreation Area
Visitors' Information: 303-728-3041

Christened for the rare tellurous ores of the region, Telluride is cupped in a granite box canyon along the San Miguel River. Area mining opened up in 1875 when John Fallon and his associate laid claim to the Sheridan, Emerald, Ausboro, and Ajax mines. A year later, J. B.

The Telluride Film Festival attracts movie buffs world-wide

Bill Ell Zey

Ingram filed a claim to the famous Smuggler and struck a vein that assayed $1,200 a ton; the gold rush was on. In its wildest days in the 1890s, Telluride had a population of more than 5,000. It was notorious for its Pacific Avenue gambling and red-light district boasting 26 saloons and 12 bordellos to service town residents. Local lore says the immorality and

Telluride Festivals

Telluride Bluegrass Festival - June
Telluride Jazz Festival - July
Telluride Film Festival - September
Telluride Hang Gliding Festival - September

isolation of Telluride caused people to warn "to-hell-u-ride," but bordellos alone contributed $1,000 in monthly fines to the town's coffers and helped keep government in business. Today, the small town of Telluride has become posh—perhaps too much so for its older residents. The area is still incredibly beautiful, but development is ongoing.

Telluride Trivia

☛ Telluride is known as the "Switzerland" of Colorado.

☛ Telluride ski area consists of 735 acres; the "plunge" is the steepest mogul run in the country.

☛ Skiing in Telluride may date back to the mid-1800s and payday at the Tomboy Mine 3,000' above town; miners are said to have skied down to beat the competition to the local brothels.

☛ **The New Sheridan Hotel** has a William Jennings Bryan Suite named for the presidential hopeful's speech of 1902; he spoke from a platform in front of the hotel.

Fairplay

Pop. 421
Elev. 9,920 ft.
Noted for: South Park City Museum; The Beach; Fairplay Hotel
Nearby: Bristlecone Pine Scenic Area; ghost towns, Pike National Forest; hot springs
Visitors' Information: 719-836-2771

Once a mining camp, Fairplay is now the largest town in the wide-open high basin county of South Park. The area was settled by Ute Indians centuries before the Spanish explorers arrived. Utes and Comanches vied for the rich hunting grounds. Trappers too were drawn here for plentiful game. The first white settlements were inspired by the gold rush of 1859. Today, Fairplay is South Park's largest town and it maintains an easygoing pace treasured by its residents.

South Park Festivals

Burro Days - July
Bayou Salado Rendezvous -
    Summer

Colo. Historical Society

Steamboat Springs was not always the bustling ski town it is today

Steamboat Springs

Pop. 5,098
Elev. 6,728 ft.
Noted for: skiing; mountain biking; Town Trail System for bikes
Nearby: Routt National Forest; hiking at Lake Dinosaur; guest ranches; Yampa River; cross-country skiing; fishing at Dumont Lake, Steamboat Lake, or Elk River
Visitors' Information: 303-879-0880

According to legend, a trio of French trappers gave Steamboat Springs its name in 1865 when they thought they heard a steamboat coming up the Yampa River. Actually, the "chhhhuuuuussssss" of the supposed water craft was created by a natural hot spring. Ten years later, James Crawford established the first white settlement on land that had been taken from the Utes by treaty in 1868. Crawford and the Utes got along so well that during the Meeker Massacre of 1879, Crawford's homestead was left alone. In 1880, the Utes were forcibly removed to a Utah reservation as the mining boom brought white hordes into the area. Although Steamboat Springs became the place for miners and cowboys to let off steam, a city "blue law" finally dried the town up and rowdies had to cross the river for a drink.

Winter Sports

In 1913, Norwegian ski champ Carl Howelsen introduced the town to recreational skiing and ski jumping. Howelsen started the Steamboat Springs tradition of **Winter Carnival**. Each February, Steamboat celebrates the winter doldrums with a week of ice-sculpting competitions, and ski jump and hockey tournaments. There's also a horsedrawn snow shovel race down Lincoln Avenue, and a parade with one of the world's only skiing high school bands.

Steamboat Springs Festivals

Winter Carnival - February
Vintage Auto Race, Concours d'Elegance - Labor Day Weekend

Trinidad

Pop. 9,663
Elev. 6,025 ft.
Noted for: Corazon de Trinidad National Historic District; Baca House and Bloom Mansion museums; Louden-Henritze Archaeology Museum; A. R. Mitchell Memorial Museum and Gallery
Nearby: Ludlow Monument; Trinidad State Recreation Area for hiking, camping, and fishing; Scenic Highway of Legends; Colorado Welcome Center: 719-846-9512
Visitors' Information: 719-846-9285

Main Street in the 1870s

Colo. Historical Society

In some ways, Trinidad feels more like New Mexico than Colorado. That's not surprising since the town sits in the shadow of Fisher's Peak less than 20 miles north of New Mexico's border. The Spanish influence is evident on your first visit. The streets of Corazon de Trinidad National Historic District are cobblestone, and many buildings are adobe or Territorial Style.

Trinidad once served as a center of commerce for area coal mines, but long before that its position at the confluence of Purgatoire River and Raton Creek made it an auspicious place to camp. The trail used by Native Americans, Spanish explorers, and Anglo traders and trappers evolved into the **Mountain Branch of the Santa Fe Trail** by the mid-1800s. In 1859, Gabriel Gutierrez established the first permanent settlement of Trinidad.

Union Blues

Twelve miles outside Trinidad, violence erupted on April 20, 1914, when a battle broke out between striking coal workers and the state militia. Several miners and two boys were killed in crossfire, and two women and 11 children perished in a fire. A monument erected by the United Mine Workers can be visited off I-25 at the Ludlow exit.

Boulder offers many opportunities for hiking

Boulder: The city rests in a valley below the Flatirons. In 1858, Captain Thomas Aikins led a party of Argonauts to settle here in what was Southern Arapaho country. The town took its name from the abundance of large boulders. In 1859, the town's first crop—turnips—was devoured by grasshoppers. The railroad arrived in 1879 . Since then, Boulder has grown into a thriving high-tech center, college town, and New Age mecca. **Noted for:** University of Colorado; Naropa Institute; Hakomi Institute; the Flatirons; Pearl Street Mall; sailplanes; Colorado Shakespeare Festival; Bolder Boulder 10K on Memorial Day weekend; tubing in Boulder Creek; hiking in Roosevelt National Forest.

Fort Collins: French trappers set up camp in 1836. Twenty-eight years later the army's Camp Collins was established and the town grew up. **Noted for:** Colorado State University; mountain biking; horseback riding; gliders; river rafting and kayaking (class IV and V) in the Cache la Poudre (don't try this without expert advice from the forest service or pro-outfitters!).

The Denver Broncos train in Greeley

Greeley: Nathan C. Meeker, agricultural editor of the *New York Tribune,* set out to create a community based on agriculture, irrigation, temperance, and religion. The town is named for the *Tribune's* editor, Horace Greeley. **Noted for:** Denver Bronco Training Camp; University of Northern Colorado; Centennial Village Museum; Meeker Home Museum.

Sterling: This small, pleasant town serves as a hub for the surrounding farm region. **Noted for:** odoriferous cattleyards; living trees sculptures; Overland Trail Museum, 303-522-3895.

Cheyenne Wells: This compact town serves as the seat of Cheyenne County and dates from the 1860s when it was a stop on the Butterfield Overland Dipatch. **Noted for:** Tumbleweed Festival.

Breckenridge: Romantic Victorian mining town. **Noted for:** public golf course designed by Jack Nicklaus; rafting; fishing.

Gunnison: Historic mining town. **Noted for:** river rafting; jeep tours; mountain biking; Pioneer Museum; ghost towns.

Crested Butte: Mining here, too. **Noted for:** National Historic District; wildflowers; golf courses.

Cortez: Human habitation of this area dates from around A.D. 1. Basketmakers and Anasazi were followed by modern farmers and, finally, tourists. Cortez is the hub for visitors to Mesa Verde National Park, Anasazi Heritage Center, Crow Canyon Archaeological Center, and Ute Mountain Tribal Park. **Noted for:** Nearby archaeological sites.

Silver Cliff: This was the major mining town during the silver boom in the late 1800s. Today, it is a service town for surrounding ranchers and farmers. **Noted for:** San Isabel National Forest and 14ers.

Georgetown: This "Silver Queen of the Rockies" had its start as a tiny mining camp in 1859. **Noted for:** Hamill House; Hotel de Paris; Georgetown Loop Narrow Gauge; Mt. Bierstadt—14,000 ft. elevation.

Golden: David Wall was the first settler here in 1858. One year later he was selling his garden produce to gold seekers at a gross of $2,000. **Noted for:** Adolph Coors Company; Colorado School of Mines.

Creede: Nicholas Creede discovered the Holy Moses Mine, and by 1892, $1 million worth of silver had been extracted from the area. **Noted for:** Commadore Mine Site in North Creede; Wheeler Geologic Area; Torchlight Ski Ceremony; Snowboarding on Table Mountain; Creede Repertory Theatre.

Cripple Creek: This was a vast cattle ranch until Bob Womack discovered gold in Poverty Gulch. **Noted for:** Cripple Creek District Museum; Cripple Creek-Victor Narrow Gauge Railroad; Florissant Fossil Beds National Monument; Mollie Kathleen Gold Mine Tour; Palace Hotel vaudeville dinner theater; Mt. Pisgah.

TASTE OF COLORADO

Standard Fare

I f you're in the mood for a taste of something different, here's a recipe that rates as a Colorado classic. Although it dates back 1,900 years, all the ingredients are still readily available in season. Of course, you can elect to purchase your rabbit at a market instead of opting for the traditional Basketmaker method of communal hunting. A rabbit was chased into a net (made of yucca and human hair) stretched 200 feet across an arroyo or canyon. Quickly, it was clubbed to death and butchered with flint tools. Because clay pots were not yet in use, the dressed rabbit was boiled in a yucca basket coated with pitch. Just in case that sounds too easy, remember you couldn't set the basket directly on an open fire. Instead, hot rocks had to be placed inside the water-filled basket. The thick taste of ashes added its own piquant flavor to this stew. The traditional method of preparation demands time and effort on your part, but when you're done, your friends will thrill to the taste of Basketmaker Rabbit Stew.

Basketmaker Rabbit Stew
1 large, fresh rabbit
1 handful wild onions
1 handful juniper berries, crushed
3 sprigs sagebrush
Boil until tender (this could take days!)

Top with this nutty sauce:
2 handfuls piñon nuts, shelled, mashed, and mixed to a paste with rain water

Serve with flat-baked, freshly ground flint corn patties. Fresh prickly pear makes a refreshing desert, but be sure to remove the spines before indulging.

Modified Rabbit

An updated version of this rabbit recipe (courtesy of the Junior League of Denver's *Creme de Colorado*) follows. Remember, rabbit is low in cholesterol.

Sautéed Rabbit

3 pounds rabbit, cut into serving pieces
3 sprigs of fresh rosemary, minced, or 1 tablespoon dried rosemary
8 fresh sage, minced, or 1 teaspoon dried sage
4 cloves garlic, minced
12 juniper berries, crushed
salt and freshly ground black pepper to taste
5 tablespoons white wine vinegar
1/2 cup olive oil
3/4 cup minced onion

Wash rabbit pieces and pat dry. In small bowl, combine rosemary, sage, garlic and juniper berries. Mix well, mashing spices together. Rub rabbit pieces with spice mixture. Season with salt and pepper. Place rabbit in large bowl. Add vinegar, olive oil and onion. Marinate, refrigerated, for 3-4 hours, turning meat several times.

Place rabbit and marinade in large, heavy kettle. Heat to boiling. Reduce heat and cover kettle. Simmer for 40-50 minutes, stirring occasionally. Increase heat to medium-high. Uncover and cook for 10-15 minutes or until meat is tender and only several tablespoons of sauce remain. Remove rabbit to heated platter. Taste and adjust seasonings in sauce. Spoon sauce over rabbit and serve immediately.

Reprinted from *Creme de Colorado* with permission from the Junior League of Denver, Denver, Colorado

Colorado's recipes have been used and improved since the days when trappers, miners, and mountain men went shopping twice a year

Get the Game Out

While hearty mountain types and gourmands might welcome the "gamey" flavor of wild game, it doesn't have to be part of your dining experience. Colorado's chefs have countless tips for getting the game out. A few of them follow. (Note: These apply to red meat or fowl.)

• Soak meat in salted water, buttermilk, milk, vinegar, or apple juice to remove blood
• Trim fat
• Refrigerate meat for at least 3 days and up to one week
• Marinades should include soy sauce, wine, vinegar, garlic, or other hearty flavors
• Serve with piquant sauces

Once you've prepared your wild game, try one of the following recipes, courtesy of the Junior League of Denver's *Colorado Cache Cook Book* and *Creme de Colorado*.

Sweet and Sour Elk Meatballs
1 pound ground elk
1/2 pound ground pork
1/2 teaspoon salt
1/4 teaspoon garlic powder
1/4 teaspoon pepper

1/4 teaspoon dried mustard
1 12-ounce jar chili sauce
1 10-ounce jar grape jelly

Place the meats in a large mixing bowl. Add salt, garlic, pepper, and mustard and knead with a fork or your hands. Shape into cocktail size balls about 1 1/2 inches in diameter. Place on a cookie sheet and bake at 350 degrees until brown, about 15 minutes. Pour the chili sauce and jelly into a large saucepan over medium heat and stir until jelly melts. Add the meatballs, a few at a time, carefully stirring to cover the meat with sauce. Continue cooking over a medium heat for about 20 minutes.

Note: This improves when prepared a few days in advance and refrigerated or frozen. Reheat at serving time in a chafing dish or serve over brown rice with a green salad as a Sunday night supper.

Reprinted from *Colorado Cache Cook Book* with permission from the Junior League of Denver, Denver, Colorado

Honey Wild Goose

1 goose (4-6 pounds)
4 teaspoons salt
2 teaspoons ground ginger
1 teaspoon freshly grated black pepper
1 1/2 cups honey
1/2 cup butter
2 teaspoons freshly grated orange peel
1/4 cup fresh orange juice
1 tablespoon fresh lemon juice
1/4 teaspoon dry mustard
2 oranges, peeled and quartered

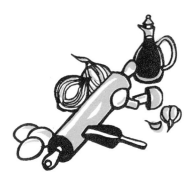

Serves: 6-8

Wash goose and soak overnight, refrigerated, in salted water to cover. Pat dry and place in roasting pan. Mix together salt, ginger, basil and pepper. Rub mixture inside cavity and over skin. In double boiler, mix together honey, butter, orange peel, orange juice, lemon juice and dry mustard. Cook until mixture becomes like syrup. Be careful not to caramelize. Coat goose body with 3 tablespoons syrup. Place oranges in cavity. Pour 1/4 cup syrup over oranges. Truss opening. Pour remaining syrup over goose. Cover with foil. Bake at 375 degrees for 2 hours. Baste 4-6 times with pan juices. After 2 hours remove foil, reduce heat to 325 degrees, and bake for an additional 30 minutes.

Reprinted from *Creme de Colorado* with permission from the Junior League of Denver, Denver, Colorado

Outdoor Dining

The key ingredient in a Colorado cookout is cooperation. The following tips are meant to be shared—and so is the work involved. And remember the first rule of recreation in the wild: Take only photographs, leave only footprints.

Tips

☛ When packing for a cookout or camping trip, choose appropriate containers to insure that cold foods stay cold and hot foods stay hot.

☛ Two drops of beach will purify eight ounces of water.

☛ Pre-measure dry ingredients for muffins, biscuits, pancakes and store in Zip-Loc baggies. Just add eggs, oil, or water to prepare.

☛ For picnics, pre-wash, dry, and tear salad greens and store in air-tight container.

☛ Break fresh eggs into a narrow-necked jar, cover, and carry; they pour out one by one.

☛ For instant barbecue flavor, sprinkle on coffee grounds as meat cooks.

☛ Keep a good supply of baking soda on hand to extinguish camp-stove fires. Add water and use the paste to brush teeth and ease burns and insect bites. This all-purpose product also serves as a pot and pan cleanser.

☛ Use only biodegradable cleansers and avoid contaminating lakes, streams, and rivers.

☛ Carry out all your garbage.

By Rank

In 1990, Colorado was number three nationally in terms of spud production. Also placing Colorado in the nation's top ten were beans, sorghum (for silage and for grain), barley, spring and winter wheat, sugar beets and corn (for silage). The state's crop production was at an all-time high during the mid-1980s. Back in the 1930s, the growing business was at a record low. ❧

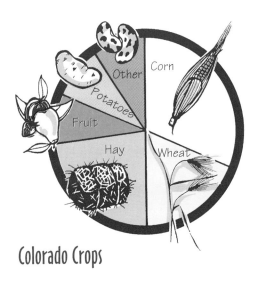

Colorado Crops

Farmer's markets offer travelers and residents a wonderful way to sample local goods in season. Weekly summer markets can be found in many communities including:
Rocky Ford, Naps Farmer's Market, 29676 E. Hwy. 50, June-October; 719-254-7483
Pueblo; 719-546-6000, ext. 3190
Denver; 303-892-1112
Boulder; 303-442-1044
Ft. Collins; 303-482-5821

Denver Metro Convention & Visitors Bureau

Colorado's Microbreweries

By definition, a microbrewery is limited in its ability to produce and distribute its beers. Some beers are only available at the brewery while others may be distributed locally, regionally, even nationally on occasion. Microbreweries only carry their own beers. Most, if not all, of the microbreweries and brew pubs offer visitors a "taster glass." This small, several-ounce glass can be used to sample several beers at very reasonable cost.

Norma Klein

Bob Klein is a beer authority from Albuquerque, New Mexico

Bob's Beer

Bob Klein is an Albuquerque freelance writer and beer aficionado. His articles about beer have appeared in magazines nationally, he is the author of a beer newsletter, and he has been a judge at sanctioned beer competitions regionally. Most importantly, as of 1992, Bob had tasted and ranked 932 different beers. The beers below are rated on a scale from 0 to 5, with 5 being the highest possible mark. A ranking of 3.5 or higher is a good beer. The listings reflect only Bob's taste buds; beer quality varies from batch to batch.

Breweries and Beer Festivals

1) Boulder Beer Co.—Boulder Boulder Extra Pale Ale-3.65. Comment: A great oak bar in the tasting room. *FYI:* 2880 Wilderness Place; 303-444-8448.

2) Coopersmith's Pub & Brewery—Fort Collins (located in a lovely brick building that was once a bakery) Horsetooth Stout-4.0. Comment: This is a gentle, classic experience of milk stout with a luscious, rich roasted malt flavor. *FYI:* 5 Old Town Square; 303-498-0483.

3) Odell Brewing Co.—Fort Collins
90 Shilling Ale-3.7. Comment: Nice citrus-fruity flavor, like grapefruit juice with malt and alcohol. Retains its fruitiness and settles into a smooth palate. Nicely integrated, light but not too fluffy. Consistent from start to finish. *FYI:* 119 Lincoln Ave; 303-498-9070.

4) Wynkoop Brew Pub—Denver
Jed Fest-3.7. Comment: Fresh and complexly flavorful. Retains an attractive fruitiness that is beguiling and a bit sweet. Not a beer for meat or heavy meals. Should accompany something lighter like fish or chicken. *FYI:* 1634 18th St.; 303-297-2700.

5) Hubcap Brewery and Kitchen—Vail
Brown and Amber Vail Pale Ale *FYI:* 303-476-5757.

6) Walnut Brewery—Boulder
This relatively new brewery serves up wheat, stout, and bitter beers. Meals are served, also. *FYI:* 1123 Walnut; 303-447-1345.

Macro Breweries

7) More than 350,000 visitors stop in Golden and take the free, 1/2-hour **Coors Brewery Tour**. This is the world's largest single brewing facility. *FYI:* Golden; 303-277-BEER.

8) Anheiseur Busch Brewery is the world's fastest-producing brewery—as many as 2,200 cans of brew per minute. Hour-long tours are free (including a visit to the Clydesdales Hamlet and those 2,300-pound beauties). *FYI:* Fort Collins; 303-490-4691.

9) Each September, Denver's Larimer Square is transformed for **Oktoberfest**. Eat, sample beer, and be merry, but choose a designated driver ahead of time. *FYI:* Denver Chamber of Commerce; 303-892-1112.

10) The Great American Beer Festival (held each October in Denver) is the place to sample Abbey Ale or old Cherry Beer from the New Belgium Brewing Co. of Fort Collins, or Amber Ale or Porter from the Boulder Brewing Co. *FYI:* 303-447-0816.

On the Vine

Most of Colorado's wineries are located at the western edge of the state in the Grand Valley, where wine grapes have been a crop for more than fifty years. Commercially, they only date to 1978. The area's clay and sand soil facilitates drainage. In grape-growing season, days are hot and dry, and nights are cool. *FYI:* Rocky Mountain Association of Vintners and Viticulturists; 303-464-0550.

All the wineries listed below welcome visitors for tasting and tours. Some are open to the public by appointment only; call ahead.

1) Colorado Cellars: The state's oldest and largest winery produces quality red, white, and blush wines. Varietals include Cabernet Sauvignon, Chardonnay, White Riesling, Cherry Wine, Merlot, and Cuvee Champagne. In 1992, their 1991 Aplenglo Riesling, 1991 Grand Valley White Riesling, and 1991 Cherry Wine all won awards at international competitions. Recommended: Grand Gamay (which has won international gold and sliver medals) and White Riesling. *FYI:* 3553 E Road, Palisade; 303-464-7921.

Wineries

2) Pikes Peak Vineyard: The winery has a tasting room, banquet facilities, and a natural outdoor amphitheater. Recommended: Riesling and Cabernet. *FYI:* Janitelle Rd., Colorado Springs; 719-576-0075.

3) Plum Creek Cellars Ltd.: They offer a full selection of wines made from Colorado-grown grapes and fruits. Recommended: Redstone Chardonnay and Grand Mesa Table Red. *FYI:* 3708 G Road, Palisade; 303-464-7586.

4) Grande River Vineyards: Chardonnay and red and white Maritage wines (those blended in the Bordeaux tradition) are specialties at this relatively young winery. *FYI:* 3708 G #2 Road, Palisade.

5) Carlson Vineyards: Plum, peach, cherry, and apple wines are featured here. Grape varieties include a wide variety of wine grapes—merlot, riesling, gewertstraminer. All their grapes are Colorado-grown. *FYI:* 461 35 Rd., Palisade; 303-464-5554.

6) Vail Valley Vintners: One of Colorado's newer wineries located in Palisade; 303-464-0559. 🐌

Grape Trivia Quiz

1) Since 1991, Colorado's Grand Valley has been a _____.
  a) designated historical site **b)** designated viticultural area
  c) designated nude bathing site

2) All Colorado wineries can sell each other's _____.
  a) labels **b)** maps **c)** products

3) Wineries can have up to ___ tasting rooms located in the state.
  a) 5 **b)** 10 **c)** 17

4) The first annual winefest was held in the town of Palisade in _____.
  a) 1981 **b)** 1989 **c)** 1992

5) A wine _____ board is appointed by Colorado's governor.
  a) tasting **b)** growers' **c)** advisory

6) The state collects a mill levy on every bottle of wine sold in Colorado to fund vineyard and winery _____.
  a) marketing **b)** safety **c)** conservation

ANSWERS: 1) b 2) c 3) a 4) c 5) c 6) a

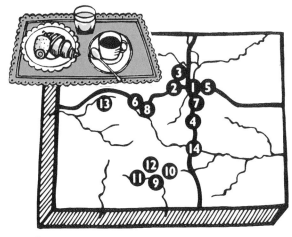

Restaurants

Dining Out

Colorado has hundreds of eating establishments and food styles to choose from, including ethnic, regional, and classic continental cuisine. The following is just a small taste of the state's restaurants.

1) La Bola, Denver: South-of-the-border fare; specialties are flautas and margaritas; 3 locations. *FYI:* 303-973-1020, 333-3888, or 779-0191.

2) Laurita's, Georgetown: In an alpine setting, dine on seafood and Italian dishes served in a family atmosphere. *FYI:* 303-776-4477.

3) Red Lion Inn, Boulder Canyon, Boulder: Bavarian style inn that specializes in veal and game. *FYI:* 303-442-9368.

4) The Broadmoor West, Charles Court, Colorado Springs: This famous hotel serves continental cuisine with a classic lake view. *FYI:* 303-577-5733.

5) The Brown Palace, Denver: Since 1892 this hotel has been serving up gold rush charm and elegance. *FYI:* 303-297-3111.

6) The Left Bank, Vail: Continental fare, casually elegant style in the nucleus of the ski area. *FYI:* 303-476-3696.

7) The Normandy, Denver: This will remind you of a French country inn and the wine cellar is exceptional. *FYI:* 303-321-3311.

8) Trapper's Cabin, Vail area: Get set to blow your wad; an evening here will cost at least $1,500. This posh log cabin—including excellent service and exceptional food—is yours for the night. *FYI:* 303-949-5750.

9) El Charro Café, Alamosa: The Mexican food here stands out from the crowd. The café is run by Ike Lucero's family and the pride of ownership is evident in the food and service. The chile is hot; no alcohol is served. *FYI:* 719-589-2262.

10) Great Sand Dunes Country Club & Inn, Great Sand Dunes: The restaurant—part of a country inn and golf course—is inside the old Zapata Ranch house. Bison, seafood, and chicken are all part of the menu. The Great Sand Dunes National Monument is minutes away. *FYI:* 719-378-2356.

11) Monte Villa Inn, Monte Vista: Great steaks, pasta, and Mexican food. Everything's comfortable, food and setting. *FYI:* 719-852-5166.

12) The Bistro, Crestone: Nourishing, filling comfort food in a lovely town. *FYI:* 719-256-4114.

13) The Village Smithy, Carbondale: baked goods, homey atmosphere. *FYI:* 303-963-9990.

14) Cornell's Country Café, Pueblo: Great home cooking in a warm country atmosphere. *FYI:* 719-542-8081. 🐌

Denver Metro Convention & Visitors Bureau

Larimer Square is a restored section of Denver's oldest street, filled with gas lamps and Victorian charm

STATE OF THE ART AND ARCHITECTURE

Art Anyone?

I f you thought Colorado was just for jocks, think again. The state is home to at least three prominent opera companies, five orchestral groups, and a dozen major art galleries.

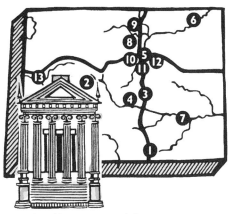

Art Museums and Centers

1) A. R. Mitchell Memorial Museum of Western Art, Trinidad: The art of traditional Western artist A. R. Mitchell is featured here. Also special exhibits of Hispanic folk art. *FYI:* 719-846-4224

2) Aspen Art Museum, Aspen: Permanent and traveling art exhibits are on display. Art classes as well as lectures, talks, tours, and concerts are offered for children and adults. *FYI:* 303-925-8050.

3) Colorado Springs Fine Arts Center, Colorado Springs: This offers visitors a prominent collection of work by Native American and Hispanic artists; Spanish colonial exhibit; sculpture, paintings, drawings by American artists. *FYI:* 719-634-5581.

4) Cripple Creek District Museum, Cripple Creek: Paintings by local artists are on display in this small, private museum. *FYI:* 719-689-2634.

5) Denver Museum of Art, Denver: This 28-sided building is a work of art housing more than 40,000 works of art and touring shows. There is also a world renowned collection of Native American artwork. *FYI:* 303-575-2793.

6) E. S. French Hall, Sterling: The works on display are by local and national artists. There is a permanent collection of William Sanderson's work. *FYI:* 303-522-3895.

7) Koshare Indian Museum, La Junta: Artifacts, and arts and crafts by Native American artists are displayed. The genesis of the museum was a 1933 Boy Scout troop project. The Koshare Indian Dance

Group—Explorer Scout Post 230—performs here also. The dances are authentic, but the dancers are non-Native Americans for the most part. *FYI:* 719-384-4411.

8) Leanin' Tree Museum of Western Art, Boulder: This museum features modern Western cowboy art as well as bronze sculptures and paintings by some of the best in the West. *FYI:* 303-530-1442.

9) Loveland Museum and Gallery, Loveland: History is prominent here, but traveling art shows are featured in the gallery. Classes and lectures are offered for kids and adults. *FYI:* 303-962-2410.

10) Museum of Western Art, Denver: The works of Frederick Remington, Charles Russell, Georgia O'Keeffe, and Albert Bierstadt are displayed here. *FYI:* 303-296-1880.

11) Trianon Museum and Art Gallery, Denver: European and Asian masterpieces from the eighteenth century are on exhibit.

12) Turner Art Gallery, Denver: Colorado's oldest art gallery was established in 1929. The paintings are from the nineteenth and twentieth centuries. There are English engravings, Colorado landscapes, and botanicals from the 1600s to the 1900s. *FYI:* 303-355-1828.

13) Western Colorado Center for the Arts, Grand Junction: The work of locally and nationally known artists is featured. *FYI:* 303-243-7339. 🐚

H. Antoine d'Arcy's poem, **"Face on the Barroom Floor,"** was inspired by a lovesick drunk's chalk drawing of "Madeline," which in turn was inspired by an 1872 poem by John Henry Titus called "Face on the Barroom Floor." Confused? There's more. Artist and newspaperman Herndon Davis actually painted a face on the barroom floor— this one at the Central City **Teller House**—in 1936. Although the Teller House (including its famous bar) has been mightily restored, the face can still be seen on the floor. *FYI:* 120 Eureka St., Central City; 303-582-3200.

Denver Metro Convention & Visitors Bureau

Art Outdoors

To avoid the usual controversy surrounding public art, Colorado artists worked with engineers and specific communities during the design stages of the **Metro Area Connection** (MAC), a new light-rail system. Ditto the **New Denver Airport Art Program**, which had its own artistic design team.

No doubt public art was controversial even in prehistoric times. Fortunately, artists sometimes prevail. **Native American Rock Art Tours** feature a close-up look at early examples of human artistic endeavors including Fremont and Ute pictographs and petroglyphs. *FYI:* 303-675-5290.

Jay Dee's Photography

Bradford Rhea with one of his living trees sculptures, "Seraphim"

Driving through Sterling, you might begin to notice trees that aren't really trees after all—they're artworks. This is the home of Brad Rhea's **"living trees" sculptures**, and these detailed works of art include a mermaid, a golfer, and giraffes. *FYI:* 800-544-8609 or 303-522-5070.

The annual **Sculpture in the Park** exhibition and show is billed as the largest exhibition of sculpture in the United States. The exhibition can be seen each August (the second weekend) at the **Benson Park Sculpture Garden** in Loveland. Many of the state's foremost sculptors live in the area or stay long enough to have their work cast by local foundries. An "Auction Under the Stars," foundry tours, and artist demonstrations are all part of the show. One-third of all sales are used to benefit the Loveland High Plains Arts Council, a nonprofit corporation. *FYI:* 303-667-6311. 🐌

In Grand Junction you can reach out and touch the state's largest display of outdoor sculpture at the city's downtown shopping park. *FYI:* **Arts on the Corner**; 303-245-2926.

Levee Art

Dave Roberts, coordinator of the **Pueblo Levee Mural Project**, was a recipient of the 1992 Governor's Awards for Excellence in the Arts. The 4 1/2-mile long, 60-foot-high levee was built to contain the waters of the Arkansas River, but under Robert's direction it is no longer the "Black Hole of Pueblo." For the last 13 years, during the Cinco de Mayo Festival, church groups, housewives, hospitalized children, and businessmen have added their artistic touch to the levee, which now functions as a public canvas. The paint is collected on "Toxic Waste Days" in Colorado Springs. This system serves as waste disposal, recycling, and a money-saving endeavor. Leftover paint goes to those in need. *FYI:* You can walk or bike along a winding levee path that will eventually lead you to the Pueblo Reservoir. A good place to pick up the path is the 4th Street Bridge.

Cynthia Ramu

A section of the Pueblo Levee Mural, which is 4¹/₂ miles long and 60 feet high

Art Workout

Once it was a working ranch; now it's a haven for working artists. **Anderson Ranch Arts Center** near Aspen offers one- and two-week summer courses for painters, woodworkers, photographers, furniture designers, and ceramic artisans. The rest of the year, a dozen artists exchange physical labor for studio space. Self-guided tours of galleries and grounds are available to the public daily, but call or write ahead for details. *FYI:* P.O. Box 5598, 5263 Owl Creek Road, 7 Snowmass Village CO 81615; 303-923-3181.

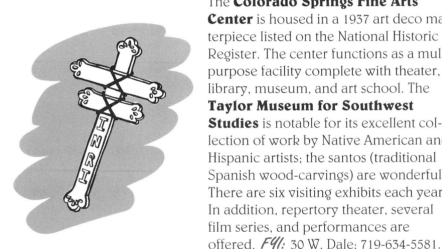

The **Colorado Springs Fine Arts Center** is housed in a 1937 art deco masterpiece listed on the National Historic Register. The center functions as a multipurpose facility complete with theater, library, museum, and art school. The **Taylor Museum for Southwest Studies** is notable for its excellent collection of work by Native American and Hispanic artists; the santos (traditional Spanish wood-carvings) are wonderful. There are six visiting exhibits each year. In addition, repertory theater, several film series, and performances are offered. *FYI:* 30 W. Dale; 719-634-5581.

Glenn Miller (1904-1944)

Born in Clarinda, Iowa, trombone player and band leader Glenn Miller was raised in Fort Morgan, Colorado, and attended the University of Colorado, Boulder, from 1924 to 1926. The Glenn Miller Band was world-famous for its swinging sound. Miller enlisted in the Air Force during WWII. He and his musicians were scheduled to play a concert in Paris when Miller's plane disappeared over the English Channel. Miller was 39 years old.

Performance

Filling four blocks at a cost of $80 million, the **Denver Performing Arts Center** complex includes six theaters, an arena, a symphony hall, and a glass arch that extends for one block. This is home to the **Denver Center Theatre Company**, the **Colorado Symphony**, and the **Colorado Ballet**. *FYI:* 303-893-3272.

Denver's **Zoofest Concert Series** is an annual musical event blending a relaxed atmosphere with eclectic musical styles—jazz, latin, blues, mandolin, and "world beat." Bring a picnic, or eat zoo fare. All proceeds benefit the non-profit Denver Zoological Foundation. Rain or shine. *FYI:* 303-892-1112.

The setting is a beautiful garden in Boulder, and the season is summer. June through mid-August the **Colorado Shakespeare Festival** performs at the Mary Rippon Outdoor Theater on the University of Colorado campus. This has been a regional attraction since 1958. *FYI:* Boulder; 303-492-8181.

In three of Colorado's outdoor amphitheaters, music lovers have the chance to hear everything from rock to classical: the 18,000-seat **Fiddler's Green Amphitheater**, Greenwood Village; **Lions Amphitheater**, Wray (*FYI:* 303-332-4737); and the acoustically near-perfect **Red Rocks Amphitheater** near Morrison (*FYI:* 303-575-2637).

Jazz in the Sangres gives you the chance to get an earful of music from some of the best jazz musicians in the country. In August since 1984—big band to fusion to blues. *FYI:* Wet Mountain Valley; 719-783-9527 or 783-9145.

Denver Metro Convention & Visitors Bureau

Red Rocks Amphitheater is a geologic wonder

Literary Colorado

Colorado's jagged peaks cut corners in the sky; almost as noticeably, they guide the shape the word takes on the page. Some of the most memorable writers use setting—an indelible sense of place—as character. Their landscapes, cities, and towns are as unforgettable as any two-legged creation roaming the pages of their books. Colorado has had its share of literary lions, and they've been exploring the state for centuries. Perhaps anyone who was bullheaded enough to traverse the Rockies 150 years ago, had the grit to write a book.

Who Said It?

"To feel the wind in your face; to ride in the teeth of a sandstorm and flying dust and furious squall; to feel the cold of dawn nip your ears and the heat of noon burn your back; to hear the thunder of the Colorado and the roar of mountain streams, and the rustle of sand through the sage, and the moan of the night breeze in the spruce, the mourn of the wolf and the whistle of the stag; to feel the silence and loneliness of the desert—all this is to grow young again."
— Zane Grey

"Of these rival cities [Denver and Auraria], Auraria is by far the more venerable—some of its structures being, I think, fully a year old. . . . Denver, on the other hand, can boast of no antiquity beyond September or October last."

— Horace Greeley

"The Platte was 'up,' they said—which made me wish I could see it when it was down, if it could look any sicker and sorrier. They said it was a dangerous stream to cross, now, because its quicksands were liable to swallow up horses, coach, and passengers if any attempt was made to ford it. But the mails had to go, and we made the attempt. Once or twice in midstream the wheels sunk into the yielding sands so threateningly that we half believed we had dreaded and avoided the sea all our lives to be shipwrecked in a "mud-wagon" in the middle of a desert at last. But we dragged through and sped away toward the setting sun."

— Mark Twain

"I jot these lines literally at Kenosha summit, where we return, afternoon, and take a long rest, 10,000 feet above sea-level. At this immense height the South Park stretches fifty miles before me. Mountainous chains and peaks in every variety of perspective, every hue of vista, fringe the view, in nearer, or middle, or far-dim distance, or fade on the horizon."

— Walt Whitman

"After much dallying and more climbing we came to a pass like all the Bolan Passes in the world, and the Black Canon of the Gunnison called they it. We had been climbing for very many hours, and attained a modest elevation of some seven or eight thousand feet above the sea, when we entered a gorge, remote from the sun, where the rocks were two thousand feet sheer, and where a rock-splintered river roared and howled ten feet below a track which seemed to have been built on the simple principle of dropping miscellaneous dirt into the river and pinning a few rails atop."

— Rudyard Kipling

The staff of The Bloomsbury Review

The Bloomsbury Review, based in Denver, is a noted literary publication and a guide to books on politics, science, travel, art, business. The *Review* also publishes the **Colorado Book Guide: A Directory of the Colorado Book Community.** *FYI:* P.O. Box 8928, Denver 80201.

Book Trivia Quiz

1) *Centennial,* one of James A. Michener's epic novels, is set in Weld County. Locals believe "Centennial" is based on the actual town of _____.

  a) Fairplay **b)** Trinidad **c)** Greeley

2) The Tattered Cover Bookstore, in Denver, is one of the largest bookstores in the country, offering readers more than _____ titles. *FYI:* 800-833-9327.

  a) 500,000 **b)** 1 million **c)** 25,000

3) Author John Naisbitt lives in Telluride. His books *Megatrends* and *Megatrends 2000* are about _____.

  a) space odysseys **b)** future trends **c)** lots of money

4) Each September, regional _____ read their work and speak about writing at the **Durango Literature Series**. Great September scenery and interesting authors. *FYI:* 303-259-3161 or 247-7496.

  a) chefs **b)** accountants **c)** writers

ANSWERS: 1) c 2) a 3) b 4) c

Film Colorado

Lights, camera, action! Between 1969 and 1991, the Colorado Film Commission spent less than one-half of 1 percent of the total monies it attracted to the state. The film industry means money wherever the action is. In 1969, the first fiscal year for the Colorado Motion Picture and Television Commission, the budget was $5,000. By 1988-89, it had blossomed to $325,000.

In odd years, the **International Invitational Poster Exhibit** offers you a chance to view an outstanding international collection of posters—including movie shots. This is a juried show and the works are judged by experts. *FYI:* Colorado State University; 303-491-6626.

Ralph Edwards (b. 1913)

Ralph Edwards, born on June 13, 1913, hails from Merino. This famous game show producer started with a radio career in 1929. He went on to produce *Truth or Consequences* (the town of Truth or Consequences in New Mexico changed its name in honor of Ralph), *This is Your Life, Place the Face, Name that Tune,* and *The People's Court.*

Denver Pyle (b. 1920)

Character actor Denver Pyle is one of those faces you don't forget. This actor from Bethune, Colorado, played roles in *Bonnie and Clyde, Life and Times of Grizzly Adams,* and *The Dukes of Hazzard.*

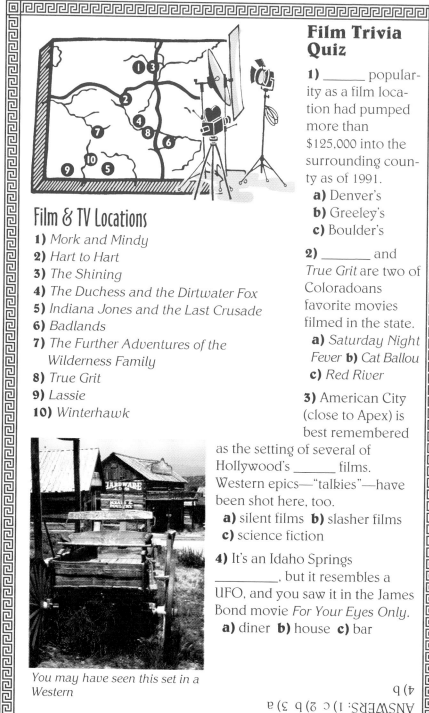

Film Trivia Quiz

1) _____ popularity as a film location had pumped more than $125,000 into the surrounding county as of 1991.

a) Denver's
b) Greeley's
c) Boulder's

2) _____ and *True Grit* are two of Coloradoans favorite movies filmed in the state.

a) *Saturday Night Fever* **b)** *Cat Ballou*
c) *Red River*

3) American City (close to Apex) is best remembered as the setting of several of Hollywood's _____ films. Western epics—"talkies"—have been shot here, too.

a) silent films **b)** slasher films
c) science fiction

4) It's an Idaho Springs _____, but it resembles a UFO, and you saw it in the James Bond movie *For Your Eyes Only*.

a) diner **b)** house **c)** bar

Film & TV Locations

1) *Mork and Mindy*
2) *Hart to Hart*
3) *The Shining*
4) *The Duchess and the Dirtwater Fox*
5) *Indiana Jones and the Last Crusade*
6) *Badlands*
7) *The Further Adventures of the Wilderness Family*
8) *True Grit*
9) *Lassie*
10) *Winterhawk*

You may have seen this set in a Western

ANSWERS: 1) c 2) b 3) a 4) b

Film Festivals

For nearly four decades, the annual **Denver International Film Festival** has screened over a hundred films and video works. This event, usually held in October, has its share of glamour, excitement, stars, and directors. *FYI:* 303-321-FILM.

Even though Aspen has a reputation as Hollywood's bedroom community, the **Aspen Filmfest** puts its spotlight on independent films rather than major studio works. The festival is usually held in September, and the selection is eclectic

The Aspen Filmfest spotlights independent films

instead of theme-oriented. John Sayles, Lily Tomlin, and Michael Lerner (of the Cohen brothers) have shown up in the past. *FYI:* 303-925-6882.

It's been called the world's best film festival, and the **Telluride Film Festival** is certainly one of the most popular. For more than twenty years, Labor Day has been the time when this mountain town celebrates the art of celluloid. Stars, filmmakers, tributes, and presentations are all part of the hubbub. There are half a dozen screens showing films simultaneously. Most of the festivals selections are world premieres, a few are classics. *FYI:* 800-525-3455.

Stacey Schiller

Building Colorado

Denver has a wealth of historic buildings, some readily visible, some tucked away on side streets. Walking tours focus on various styles and subjects, including Mansions and Millionaires or Lower Downtown. *FYI:* **Historic Denver Inc.**

The **Biennial Summer Victorian House Tour** gives you access to better Victorian homes and gardens. This is a one-day affair. If you miss it this year, you'll have to wait two more years. *FYI:* Georgetown Society; 303-569-2840, or in Denver, 303-674-2625.

Colorado Historical Society

The Brown Palace

Denver's best known hotel, the **Brown Palace**, opened in 1892. This Victorian masterpiece is constructed of Colorado red granite and Arizona sandstone. Inside, wrought iron balconies rise six stories to a stained-glass ceiling. Guests have a breathtaking view of the lobby where afternoon tea is served. The Palace has a reputation for immaculate service and luxurious accommodations. Each room is different and many of the bathrooms are art deco style. *FYI:* 800-321-2599 nationwide; 800-228-2917 in state.

Colo. Historical Society

Molly Brown (1867–1932)

Molly Brown, one of Colorado's outstanding characters, survived the sinking of the Titanic and eventually inspired the musical *The Unsinkable Molly Brown*. Molly's husband, J. J. Brown, made his fortune from the Little Johnny gold mine. Together, they lived in a mansion built in 1889 by famous Denver architect William Lang. Today, tours are given of the turn-of-the-century lace, wood, and velvet interior. *FYI:* 303-832-4092.

The **Castle Marne** is one of Denver's finest historic inns. The stone building dates to 1889, and it was designed by one of the state's more eclectic architects, William Lang (who also designed the Molly Brown house). The building suffered through a time of neglect, but recent renovations by the current owners show off hand-hewn stonework, woodwork, balconies, and the great turret. *FYI:* 303-331-0621.

For a view of Denver's more modern architecture, visit the four-square-block **Denver Performing Arts Complex**. The complex includes the **Boettcher Concert Hall** (home of the Colorado Symphony Orchestra) as well as the **Auditorium Theatre** (where the Denver Center Theatre Company and the Colorado Ballet are in residence). *FYI:* 303-640-2862.

Denver Metro Convention & Visitors Bureau

Denver Performing Arts Complex

Colorado Historical Society

The Broadmoor Hotel

The Broadmoor

Privileged turn-of-the-century newcomers to the Colorado Springs area included the Baldwins of Newport and New York. They hired architect Stanford White to design a residence in classic style. White sketched preliminary plans before his death in 1905. Architect Thomas MacLaren, who took over for White, traveled to France to scrutinize the Grand Trianon at Versailles before he designed the Baldwins' Broadmoor estate.

Gold and copper entrepreneur Spencer Penrose purchased the property in 1916 and opened a luxury resort. Today, the Broadmoor is a five-star resort set at the base of Cheyenne Mountain. The facility includes three hotels, luxury shops, golf courses, tennis courts, a ski area, and three spring-fed pools. Black swans may be seen in the lake that separates the most modern Broadmoor from the older hotels. *FYI:* 719-634-7711.

Silverton's **Teller House** hotel dates to 1872; since that time, it has continued to provide fine dining and accommodations for world-weary travelers. The original construction was completed at a cost of about $107,000. A special walkway made of silver bars was created for President Ulysses S. Grant's visit in 1873. In 1932, the **Teller Opera House** was reopened. Tours are conducted daily. *FYI:* 303-582-3200.

Lillian Gish, Faye Emerson, Helen Hayes, Edwin Booth, Sarah Bernhardt, and Shirley Booth all once performed at the **Central City Opera House**. The building was dedicated in 1878, and the interior is still graced with crystal chandeliers and colorful murals. *FYI:* 303-582-5202.

Denver Metro Convention & Visitors Bureau

The contemporary architecture of the *Air Force Academy* in Colorado Springs makes it a favorite of locals and visitors alike

The **Navarre Building**, constructed in 1889, was once Denver's classiest bordello and gambling hall. Today, it is the home of the Museum of Western Art, one of the nation's finest Western art collections, with 125 paintings and sculptures.

Gardens

Settler and pharmacist Walter Cheesman built a turn-of-the-century hor
for his family in Denver. He died before it was completed; nevertheless,
left a garden legacy that equaled the best gardens of Europe. In 1926, Mr
Cheesman sold the house to Claude Boettcher. Charles Boettcher,
Claude's father, had single-handedly founded Colorado's sugar beet
industry when he returned from Europe with a bounty of seeds.
Eventually, the Boettcher family donated the home to the state; it becan
the **Governor's Mansion**. Today, half-hour tours are offered on a limit
basis. *FYI:* 303-866-3682.

The great glass honeycomb conservatory at the **Denver Botanic
Gardens** encloses a tropical forest that includes cocoa, banana, and
carob trees. There is a lush orchid room, a peaceful Japanese garden, an
alpine gardens (best visited in May and June). Other floral attractions
include roses, water lilies, an herb garden, and a Plants of the Bible garden. Often, on summer nights folks gather here to enjoy concerts in the
amphitheater. On the trivial side, Woody Allen's film *Sleeper* was filmed i
the Denver Botanic Gardens. *FYI:* 303-331-4010.

Washington Park is graced by great trees, wide lawns, and several
lakes. Kids and adults swim (in the indoor pool), fish, hike, and play here
springtime is the favorite season for locals. There's volleyball, horseshoes
bicycling, rollerskating, and a handicap-accessible playground. But gar-
deners should spend time on the park's west side at Downing Street,
where flowers bloom in technicolor. On the north bank of Grasmere
Lake, look for the replica of George Washington's Garden at Mt. Vernon.
FYI: Denver, between Louisiana and Virginia avenues.

Denver's **City Park** was created
by the designer of London's Hyc
Park and Munich's English
Gardens. A rose garden graces
the park's east side. Grassy spac
and tall trees remind you that
green areas are a boon to any
city. Paddle boats are for rent at
one of City Park's lakes. *FYI:*
Denver, between Colorado Blvc
and York Street.

The original **Elitch Gardens** were planted in 1890 by Denver's Mary Elitch. She offered free concerts for children and gave them access to classical music. Today, Elitch Gardens is an amusement park with its own world-famous roller coaster. There are still flowers to be seen. *FYI:* 303-455-4771.

The floral clock at Denver's Elitch Gardens

THE SPORTING LIFE

Telluride Ski Resort/T.R. Youngstrom

Snowboarding is the hot new winter sport

Cold Sports

Each year, 10 million skiers are drawn to Colorado's 23,000 ski-able acres and the slopes of its 27 major ski resorts. They find an extended ski season, excellent snow conditions, state-of-the-art snow-making capabilities, and the high altitudes that make those long runs possible. *FYI:* Colorado Ski Country U.S.A., 1560 Broadway, Suite 1440, Denver, CO 80202; 303-837-0793.

Military Skis

In the early phases of World War II, the Russians invaded Finland and the Germans invaded Norway—both were brutal winter forays—and it became clear to the allies that there was a need for an elite American corp of combat skiers. In 1941, the U.S. Army selected a mountain site 25 miles south of Vail and 18 miles north of Leadville as the training ground of the **10th Mountain Division**.

Camp Hale (nicknamed "Camp Hell" because of its 9,480 foot elevation) was cold, snowy, and rough on the 15,000 members of the 87th Mountain Infantry (future 10th Mountain Divisioners), who began arriving in the fall of 1942.

Aspen's Jerome Hotel was the watering hole of choice for thirsty trainees. A soda fountain graced the bar of the Jerome, and Camp Hale's temporary refugees invented "Aspen Crud," a bourbon milk-shake. The 10th Mountain Division completed their training and left for combat in Italy. Today, the names of almost 1,000 men who died in combat are etched in a 20-foot high granite block. *FYI:* Aspen; 303-925-1940. 🐾

Trail Systems

1) San Juan Hut System: This connects Telluride, Ridgway, and Ouray over 56 miles with five back country ski huts. The route tracks the Dallas and Alder Creek Trains in the Mt. Sneffels Range of the San Juan Mountains. The huts are accessible to all level skiers while more advanced terrain awaits powder hounds above the huts. *FYI:* San Juan Hut Systems, Box 1663, Telluride, CO 81435; 303-728-6935.

2) 10th Mountain Trail Association Hut System: It was organized in 1980 in honor of the ski troops who trained in the area for combat in WWII. More than 250 miles of trails and ten huts connect Leadville, Aspen, and Vail. The trail will eventually hook up Aspen and Vail Pass. *FYI:* 10th Mountain Trail Assoc., 1280 Ute Ave., Aspen, CO 81611; 303-925-5775.

3) Silver City Trail: Ski Leadville's mining district but stay on the roads to avoid deadly pits and holes. *FYI:* Leadville Chamber of Commerce, 809 Harrison Ave.; 719-486-3900.

4) Never Summer Nordic Yurt System: Nomadic Turks carried their yurts—dome-shaped portables—with them as they trekked cross country. This yurt system is located in the Medicine Bow Range and Never Summer Mountains of the Colorado State Forest. The yurts sleep six and even boast a sun deck. Rates are reasonable, reservations crucial. *FYI:* Never Summer Nordic, P. O. Box 1254, Fort Collins 80522; 303-484-3903.

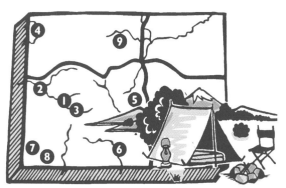

No matter your pleasure, there's a recreation area to suit in Colorado

USDA Forest Service

Public Lands

Two national parks, five national monuments, two national grasslands, 12 national forests, more than 20 wilderness areas, 40 state parks and recreation areas, and acres of BLM land have been set aside for recreational use and conservation in Colorado. *FYI:* National Park Service: 303-969-2000. National Forest Service: 303-236-9431. Bureau of Land Management: 303-239-3600

1) Black Canyon of the Gunnison National Monument: A breathtaking 2,000-foot sheer rock canyon cut by the Gunnison River over a 2-million-year span. Hiking, horseback riding, mountain climbing. *FYI:* 303-249-7036.

2) Colorado National Monument: Spires, columns, and canyons. Bicycling, hiking, mountain climbing, horseback riding, cross-country skiing. *FYI:* 303-858-3617.

3) Curecanti National Recreation Area: Colorado's largest body of water, Blue Mesa Reservoir, and two other lakes are situated on this 60-mile-long area. Boating, hiking, mountain climbing, swimming, snowmobiling, and cross-country skiing. *FYI:* 303-641-2337.

4) Dinosaur National Monument: A world-famous dinosaur fossil quarry, breathtaking vistas, Fremont prehistoric sites, and river rafting in 211,085 acres of the monument. Mountain climbing, boating, hiking. *FYI:* 303-374-2216.

5) Florissant Fossil Beds National Monument: A volcanic eruption 35 million years ago buried and preserved insect, plant, and fish fossils. Cross-country skiing, mountain climbing. *FYI:* 719-748-3253.

National Parks & Monuments

6) Great Sand Dunes National Monument: Five-hundred-sixty-five square miles of sand and dunes reaching heights of more than 1,000 feet. Hiking, mountain climbing. *FYI:* 719-378-2312.

7) Hovenweep National Monument: Canyon heads and six clusters of dwellings dating back 900 years. Hiking, mountain climbing.

8) Mesa Verde National Park: Fifty-two thousand acres and more than 4,000 archaeological sites. Hiking. *FYI:* 303-529-4461.

9) Rocky Mountain National Park: Streams, valleys, mountain lakes are all part of the state's largest national park. There are 113 peaks more than 10,000 feet above sea level and 78 peaks over 12,000 feet. Horseback riding, hiking, mountain climbing, cross-country skiing, snowmobiling. *FYI:* 303-586-2371. 🐎

Llamas, anyone?

If your own two feet are overworked, you might entertain the thought of letting a four-legged member of the Camelid family carry your burden. These guys are strong, sure-footed, and they won't talk your ear off. Indigenous to the South American Andes, llamas have been beasts of burden for more than 3,500 years. Although North American llamas might seem a bit trendy, fossil records show that their ancestors cruised Colorado, New Mexico, Arizona, and Utah very long ago. They're back, and they're great packers. *FYI:* Colorado Llama Outfitters and Guides Association; P. O. Box 1394, Carbondale 81623.

Sangre de Cristo Wilderness Adventures

Recreational Trivia Quiz

1) How much of Colorado's 104,651 square miles is public land?
 a) less than half **b)** half **c)** more than half
2) Colorado has ____ state parks.
 a) 40 **b)** 31 **c)** 44
3) There are ___ species classified as sport game in the state.
 a) 78 **b)** 99 **c)** 113

ANSWERS: 1) c 2) a 3) c

14ers!

Get a good start on becoming a 14er—someone who has climbed all of the state's peaks over 14,000 feet elevation—by hiking three in one day! Mounts Democrat (14,148 feet), Lincoln (14,286 feet), and Bross (14,169 feet) can all be scaled by following a 6-mile loop trail. This is for the conditioned; the overall elevation gain is more than 3,500 feet. *FYI:* The trailhead is at Kite Lake, 7 miles from Alma via Buckskin Gulch.

Mt. of the Holy Cross is one of the 53 peaks over 14,000 feet in Colorado

Peaks

Whatever men can do, women can do as well or better. This is the basic principle of the **Colorado Mountain Club**, which was founded in 1912. Julia Holmes proved it on Pikes Peak in 1858; so did Anna Dickinson and Isabella Bird when they reached the summit of Long's Peak in 1873. Famous female members of the club include Dr. Florence Sabin, who created Colorado's health code, and Mary Cronin, the first woman to climb all 51 14ers (in 1921 it was 51 peaks; now the United States Geological Survey puts the total at 53), and Agnes Vaille, who froze to death on Long's Peak on January 12, 1925 after ascending the extremely difficult and dangerous East Face. Members of the club are conservationists who uphold Henry Thoreau's belief that the best environment is a balance of wilderness and civilization. The club has advocated preservation since its founding. *FYI:* for info on mountain climbing, 303-922-8315.

Expert and novice **rock climbers** can choose from more than ten sites in Telluride and surrounds. Whether you are bouldering, top-roping, or lead climbing, do it under expert supervision only. *FYI:* 303-728-3041.

The 7,000-foot-high **Spanish Peaks** were a welcome landmark to travelers along the Santa Fe Trail. Tucked between the peaks and the Sangre De Cristos is the **Cuchara Valley** where the culture is still a rich mixture of Hispanic and Anglo, south and west. This valley was once part of a Spanish land grant. Today, **San Isabel National Forest** belts the valley from mountain range to peaks.

If you're bored with the usual winter recreational fare, why not try **ice climbing**? Your target is one of winter's frozen-solid waterfalls. You need two-fisted axes and ice screws on the hip. The Ouray area is a popular ice climbers playground. *FYI:* 303-325-4746. 🐌

Julia Archibald Holmes (1838–1887)

The westward rush for gold brought a steady stream of hopefuls to Colorado and California in the 1850s. Among these pioneer parties was a group of 49 people who left Lawrence, Kansas, in 1858. Julia Archibald Holmes, a 22-year-old bride, was one of two women on the trip. Her style of reform dress—calico skirts to the knees and bloomers below—didn't please the males, but Julia made it clear she dressed for her own happiness and comfort. When her party reached the base of Pikes Peak, Julia discovered few men—and certainly no women—had ever climbed to the summit. She promptly and easily made it to the top with her husband and two other men on August 5, 1858. News spread and American women were inspired. Julia was proof that women have always fared at least as well as men in their endeavors—especially on the arduous pioneer trail. The challenge of Pikes Peak still exists 150 years later. Backcountry hiking is one of the best (and it can be one of the least intrusive) ways to prove your mettle and explore public lands. *FYI:* U.S. Forest Service, P.O. Box 25127, 11177 W. 8th Ave, Lakewood, CO 80225.

There are more than 2,000 lakes and reservoirs open to fishing in Colorado

Go Fish

Bait your hook, tie your fly! There are 65,000-plus miles of streams and more than 2,000 lakes and reservoirs open to fishing. *FYI:* Division of Wildlife; 303-249-3431.

1) Silver Jack Reservoir: (northeast of Ouray) Good for rainbow trout in spring and fall. Also try for brook and cutthroat.
2) Molas and Little Molas: (near Silverton) Compact but lively trout.
3) Island Lake: (near Silverton) Good trout fishing.

4) Andrews: (near Silverton) Not too much traffic and good for cutthroat.
5) Woods Lake: (near Telluride) Near the base of three 14ers. The rainbow, cutthroat, and brook trout fishing is good; only artificial flies and lures permitted.
6) Little Ice Lake: (near Silverton) Cutthroat trout.
7) Clear Lake: (near Silverton) Cutthroat trout.
8) Peacock Pool: (Estes Park) You need to hike into the water to hook the 8" cutthroat.

Lake Fishing

9) Grand Lake and **Shadow Mountain Lake:** (Grand Lake) These lakes are the site of the AnnualFish Derby.

10) Lake Granby: (Grand Lake) Rainbow, kokanee, and big brown trout.

11) McPhee Reservoir: (Cortez) Stocked trout, large- and small-mouth bass, bluegills, and crappie.

12) Ground Hog Reservoir: (Cortez) Twelve-inch trout are best caught from boats.

13) Queens State Wildlife Area: (Near Lamar) Nee Noshe, Nee So Pah, Nee Grande, and Nee Shaw hold perch, walleye, perch, bass, and catfish. Springtime is the best time to cast. 🎣

Set Sail

Sailing, river floats, water-skiing, even yacht races can all be found in Colorado. **Lake Dillon** is a great place to set sail. The Lake Dillon Marina facility offers rental fish boats, sail boats, and dinner floats. *FYI:* 303-668-5800 or 303-468-5400.

Pueblo Reservoir, a few miles west of Pueblo, is the spot to hoist your sail (small to medium craft), and it's a great favorite with windsurfers of all levels. (Sorry, no rentals). *FYI:* North Marina; 719-547-3880.

Sailing at Lake Dillon

L. Carr/USDA Forest Service

Fish Trivia Quiz

1) How many miles of Colorado's steams are classified as "Gold Medal" quality? **a)** 321 **b)** 158 **c)** 23

2) The annual fishing license fee for nonresidents in 1992 was _____.

a) $20.25 **b)** $32.50 **c)** $40.25

3) Colorado has more than ____ fishable lakes and reservoirs that are open to the public.

a) 2,000 **b)** 3,000 **c)** 4,500

4) Almost 150 miles of streams and more than 550 surface acres of lakes in Colorado are classified _____. **a)** 20" Limit Waters **b)** Special Limit Waters **c)** Wild Trout Waters

ANSWERS: 1) b 2) c 3) a 4) c

Duane Davey/USDA Forest Service

Biking near Lost Lake Slough, Gunnison National Forest

Set the Pace

Racing—on your own two feet, four feet, two wheels, in the air, or in water—is big sport in Colorado. If all that sounds "ho hum" to you, maybe hot-air balloon rodeos or a dog-sled trip will suit your fancy. Most towns have local guides, teachers, and experts, as well as rental equipment. They also have special festivals.

Winterskol has been part of January in Aspen since 1952. Ski races top off five days of partying. There's a drink-mixing competition, fireworks, and lovely torchlit mountain descents. *FYI:* Aspen; 303-925-1940.

Snowmass Balloon Festival bills itself as the world's biggest high-altitude balloon fest. Balloons are the oldest form of air transportation, but these competitors bring the very latest skills to survive tests of speed and dexterity. *FYI:* Aspen; 303-923-2000.

Krabloonik's Kennels offers half- and full-day sled trips into the Maroon Bells-Snowmass Wilderness Area. Dog-sled teams in the Aspen area date back to 1947 when they were trained for the 10th Mountain Division during WWII. These days, Krabloonik's is one of the largest kennels of its kind. Rides are for pleasure, and they are expensive. *FYI:* Aspen; 303-923-3953.

Strawberry Days, the state's oldest municipal fest, has been celebrated in Glenwood Springs since 1898. Races include a 5K, a 10K, and a pony express ride. Strawberries and ice cream are always on hand. *FYI:* Glenwood Springs; 303-945-6589.

Rainbow Weekend, Steamboat Springs, is one of the few spots where you can take a ride in a hot-air balloon each July. Events include roping a "steer" from a balloon. *FYI:* 303-879-0880.

Rainbow Trail Round-Up Mountain Bike Race in Westcliffe is only for serious competitors. It's a harsh, haul-ass ride from Westcliffe on the Rainbow Trail. *FYI:* 719-783-9163.

Bolder Boulder 10K is the place to line up each Memorial Day with thousands of other entrants. *FYI:* 303-442-1044. 🚲

❶ **Tenmile Canyon Bikeway**

❷ **Blue River Bikeway**

Bike Trails

Two-Wheelers

Colorado is crisscrossed by old mining and logging roads, many of them navigable by mountain bike. A wide-tire, 15-gear, alloy frame bike is perfect for the roads around Durango, Steamboat Springs, and Crested Butte.

San Juan Hut System (connecting Telluride, Colorado, to Moab, Utah) is made for bikes or skis, in season. *FYI:* 303-728-6935.

Colorado National Monument has very long, very beautiful bike trails. *FYI:* 303-858-3617.

Kokopelli's Trail—128 miles between Loma and Moab, Utah—has only been officially open since 1989. The going is rugged and the scenery is breathtaking. Kokopelli is the hump-backed flute player of Native American lore. *FYI:* Colorado Plateau Mountain Bike Trail Association, P.O. Box 4602, Grand Junction, 81502; 303-241-9561.

Miles of paved bikeways in Summit County mean you can whiz along the 9-mile **Blue River Bikeway** between Breckenridge and Frisco or cruise the 6-mile **Tenmile Canyon Bikeway** between Copper Mountain and Vail—and that's just for starters. Unpaved jeep roads in the area are also bikeable. All wilderness areas are off-limits to bikes. *FYI:* Dillon Ranger District Office, 135 Hwy. 9, P.O. Box 620, Silverthorne, 80498; 303-468-5400.

USDA Forest Service

Eaglets waiting for a snack

For the Birds

The San Luis Valley has gone to the birds, and that's great news for birders. Marshlands along the Rio Grande River attract migratory teals, avocets, and sandhill and whooping cranes. This is also winter territory for raptors such as hawks, golden eagles, and bald eagles. The U.S. Fish and Wildlife Service maintains a self-guided loop drive through the **Alamosa-Monte Vista National Wildlife Refuge**. *FYI:* Refuge Manager, Alamosa-Monte Vista National Wildlife Refuge, P.O. Box 1148, Alamosa 81101; 719-589-4021.

The San Luis Valley is a major bird fly-way. Each March, the town of Monte Vista celebrates the **Crane Festival** to honor the birds visiting nearby Alamosa-Monte Vista National Wildlife Refuge. Town events are geared for fun and for educating the public about wet-lands. *FYI:* Monte Vista Chamber of Commerce; 719-852-2731.

Rodeo Fever

Colorado is rodeo land and Denver is at the heart of the nation's professional rodeo circuit. The Mile-High City boasts the state's largest purse for professional

Colorado is rodeo land

competition: $101,500. Statewide, there are more than fifty pro rodeos to be seen between the months of January and September. Local amateur competitions are too numerous to list, but contact the chamber of commerce in the area you plan to visit for information. For a complete listing of Professional Rodeo Cowboys Association rodeos and events, contact the PRCA; 719-593-8840.

Push Comes to Shove

Organized **pack burro racing** began in 1949, but the roots of the sport reach all the way back to the 1800s when a miner and his burro depended on each other for survival. By nature, burros can be stubborn, cantankerous, and downright ornery. These are the qualities that modern-day burro racers must contend with. Colorado's "Triple Crown" takes place in Fairplay, Leadville, and Buena Vista in that order. A team of human and beast is timed from start to finish—downtown Buena Vista. During the entire race they must run side by side cross-country. *FYI:* The Buena Vista Pack Burro Racing Association, Inc., P.O. Box 1428, Buena Vista, CO 81211. 🐌

Stock Trivia

☛ For more than one hundred years, cowboys have been toughing it out at the July 4th Meeker rodeo, which is part of **Range Call**. Events are for professionals, and the last day is for local ranch hands only. *FYI:* 303-878-5510.

☛ Most weeks, June through August, ranch hands in the Steamboat Springs area can be seen busting and roping and dogging. This is the nation's biggest pro rodeo—the **Weekly Rodeo**—and it's held at the Steamboat Rodeo Grounds. *FYI:* 303-879-0880.

☛ More than 400,000 visitors from all over North America flock to Denver to the **National Western Stock Show**. *FYI:* 303-297-1166.

☛ **Ski-Hi Stampede** is a three-day pro rodeo that's been in business since 1921. In addition to bronc busting and bulldogging, a carnival and chuckwagon dinner are part of the ruckus. *FYI:* Monte Vista; 719-852-2055.

USDA Forest Service

Coloradoans know how to relax

At Play

Recreation, anyone? In Colorado, it's a way of life as well as a liveli-hood. Some of the state's more interesting present-day recreational activities took their origins from the bond between miner and beast-of-burden (burro racing) or from discovering the fastest way to travel downhill from goldmine to bordello (on skis, of course).

Hunting

Colorado hunters may legally pursue elk, mule deer, big horn sheep, and pronghorn antelope in season. The state classifies 113 species of wildlife as sport game. License fees vary. *FYI:* Colorado Department of Natural Resources, 6060 Broadway, Denver 80216-1000; 303-297-1192.

Golf

When it's time to tee off, some of Colorado's golf courses measure up to the best the nation has to offer. Golfing in the Rockies presents pros and novices special challenges—the ter-rain is difficult and balls travel farther. For information on celebrity and PGA tourna-ments, and courses in general, contact: **Colorado Golf Association**, Suite 101, 5655 S. Yosemite, Englewood, 80111; 303-779-GOLF or 800-228-4675.

Arthur H. Carhart (1892–1978)

Conservationist Arthur H. Carhart, a young Forest Service employee, convinced the Department of Agriculture not to develop Trappers Lake and its White River environs. Up to this point, roads and development were permitted in National Parks. Preservation lulled until the 1950s when the Sierra Club and the Wilderness Society were active in the Echo Park dam controversy which resulted in the 1964 passage by Congress of the National Wilderness Preservation Bill.

Colo. Historical Society

Sports Trivia

☞ **Denver Broncos** work out at the University of Northern Colorado at Greeley during summer months. You can usually get an autograph, and the public is welcome to view most events.

USDA Forest Service

Windsurfing is a popular sport in Colorado

☞ The headquarters of the **U.S. Olympic Training Center** in Colorado Springs trains an average of 125,000 athletes each year.

☞ The 1990 mountain **biking world championships** were held in Durango.

☞ Bikers and hikers have their very own campground at **Peninsula Recreation Area** in Summit County. No motor vehicles allowed.

☞ **Winter Park** (near Breckenridge) has more than 500 miles of marked trails, and it's one of the state's mountain biking hot spots.

☞ If you try windsurfing at **Ruedi Reservoir** (Aspen), bring your wet-suit no matter what the season.

SPIRIT OF COLORADO

Healthy Soaks

Anasazi farmers, Ute chiefs, Spanish conquistadores, gamblers and gunslingers, movie stars, health freaks, and presidents have all soaked in Colorado's healing mineral spring waters. Facilities range from au naturel to resort spiffy. Call ahead when possible, to make reservations and verify seasonal specifics.

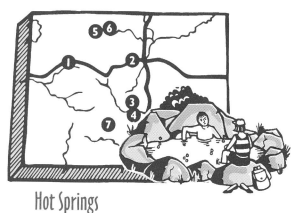

Hot Springs

1) Glenwood Hot Springs Pool: This is billed as the world's largest outdoor mineral hot springs pool. The resort was built in the 1880s, and the upper crust took advantage of the waters and the pampering at the famous Hotel Colorado. Astors, Vanderbilts, and even Al Capone stayed here. At one time, Glenwood played host to desperado dentist Doc Holliday. The 615-foot by 75-foot brick-lined pool was finished in 1888, labor courtesy of the inmates of the local jail. *FYI:* 303-945-7131.

2) Indian Springs Resort: Historically, these springs were a neutral area for various Native American tribes who shared their soothing effects. Miners, artists (Walt Whitman), and even a president (Teddy Roosevelt) indulged here. Today, skiers are the most frequent visitors. In addition to mineral baths, you can explore Club Mud and vapor caves. The facility is a bit run-down. There are overnight facilities. *FYI:* Idaho Springs; 303-567-2191.

3) Mount Princeton Hot Springs Resort: This offers visitors a terrific trio—nice lodgings, good eats, and hot springs. The original building, which met the needs of the rich and famous, has been torn down, but the new lodge does just fine. You can soak in- or outdoors. The exterior rock pools were built by a New Age group during the Harmonic Convergence. *FYI:* Nathrop; 719-395-2447.

4) Salida Hot Springs: Thank the WPA and 1937 for the largest indoor hot springs pool—25 meter lap and wading pools—in the state; the water is piped an 8-mile distance. This facility is in good shape and private tubs are available. *FYI:* Salida; 719-539-6738.

5) Steamboat Springs Health and Recreation Association: Assorted 100-degree pools and a hydro water slide await the needy. This is a family-oriented soak. *FYI:* Steamboat Springs; 303-879-1828.

6) Strawberry Park Natural Hot Springs: Rock-lined pools, here—between 104 and 150 degrees. Suits optional after dark. Varied overnight accommodations. *FYI:* Steamboat Springs; 303-879-0342.

7) Valley View Hot Springs: You're welcome to soak and relax in these natural mineral pools located on the west slope of the Sangre de Cristo Mountains on any weekday (weekends are for members only). Bathing suits are optional and you can choose from developed or natural pools. Overnight accommodations are not expensive, but you should bring your own bedding. *FYI:* Villa Grove; 719-256-4315. 🐚

Hot Trivia

☛ Mineral Hot Springs (located in the San Luis Valley) was cursed by the Ute Indians, who predicted its economic failure. If you don't believe in curses, try to ignore the fact that Mineral Hot Springs subsequently went dry.

☛ The Utes believed that Glenwood Hot Springs—they called it Yampah, "Big Medicine"—was of spiritual importance, and they valued it for its healing powers.

Los Hermanos

In remote portions of northern New Mexico and southern Colorado, members of the lay order commonly known as **Los Hermanos Penitentes**, the Penitente Brothers, still practice religious customs that date back to the early 1800s.

Although they have been replaced for the most part with milder forms of penance, self-flagellation and simulated crucifixions were common in early days. During Lent, brothers left the *moradas* (Penitente meeting houses), some engaging in strenuous physical penance, all wearing black hoods and white trousers, and marched to the *Calvario*, the cross. Los Hermanos were often a cohesive influence in the community, and they practiced acts of charity.

By the end of the nineteenth century, the Brothers were in conflict with the Catholic Church. For protection, secrecy became an important part of Penitente ritual, and the practices of Holy Week in a morada are still very private.

Moradas are often found at the edge of a village, and they look much like small chapels with fewer windows. Although Colorado had hundreds of moradas 85 years ago, there are only a few today. These can be seen in some of Southern Colorado's Hispanic villages. These are very private places of worship, and you should not intrude.

Treasure Hunt

Overlooking Wet Mountain Valley, **La Caverna del Oro** (Gold Cavern a.k.a. Spanish Cave) is tucked high in the Sangre de Cristo Mountains. La Caverna del Oro is a caver's nightmare, accessible only one month out of the year (the snow melts in August and falls in September), dank, dark, and filled with steep shafts and tunnels. Spanish explorers heard a tale or two about this formidable cave when they first arrived in the sixteenth century. As one story goes, Indians had discovered gold and offered it to their gods. Somehow, the spirits were angered and mining ceased. A second story relates the journey of Spanish monks who uncovered the cave on an excursion north from Mexico and New Mexico. Friendly local Indians were then betrayed by the *padre* and forced into slavery. Eventually, the Indians were slaughtered. Yet another version of this story implies that the Spaniards were forced to defend themselves from inside the cave, where they constructed a rudimentary fort. Ultimately, the Spaniards took the gold back to Mexico.

In 1811, a Spanish-American is said to have discovered nuggets and gold bricks in the mountains. More than fifty years later, Elisha Horn just may have found a skeleton sporting Spanish armor on Marble Mountain. There was more news of the cave in 1880 when J. H. Yoeman stumbled on the entrance and an old fortress, which gave some credence to the early legends. In 1920, forest rangers found La Caverna del Oro after listening to a descendant of the first Spanish explorers, Mrs. Apollina Apodaca. They found a Maltese cross painted on rock and felt a frigid wind coming from the cave's depths.

In 1929, a cave expedition told of finding logs, and an old chain ladder, but no traces of gold. A few years later, another expedition reported a skeleton chained to a stone wall. Soon after, Dr. LeRoy Hafen, curator of the Colorado State Historical Society was hoisted into the shaft. He spied not a bone, but he did retrieve some seventeenth century artifacts.

Later stories only add to the mystery. Some have seen odd, eerie lights at night near the entrance. The ghost of a crucified trapper is said to haunt the cold, dreary cave. A human bone was found; so were bundles of dynamite. And perhaps most significant of all is the fact that cavers have very bad luck in La Caverna del Oro. Of course, the gold—if it exists—has yet to be discovered.

Ghost Treasure

Near the Old West ghost town of St. Elmo, many have risked their lives looking for treasure after hearing a long, tall tale. As the story goes, Spanish conquistadores cached their booty of gold and silver at the base of the Chalk Cliffs on the south face of Mt. Princeton. These limestone cliffs are rugged and deadly if you put your foot in the wrong spot. For a safer expedition, check out the weathered remains of St. Elmo, a town that dates back to 1880.

Grave Business

For those spirited souls who like to wander and browse through cemeteries, Colorado offers lots of grave opportunites. Many of the ornate headstones and wrought iron fences you'll find date back to Victorian times. Simpler markers demonstrate human ingenuity when times and wallets were lean but someone had to be buried. Please be considerate when you explore graveyards, and never remove or deface property.

For fans of the Old West, **Linwood Cemetery**, Glenwood, is a must. The second corpse to be laid in the ground here belonged to the notorious gambler, dentist, and shootist Doc Holliday. Doc came to Glenwood in 1887 to find a cure for his tuberculosis. No such luck. He died in November of the same year at the age of 35. A simple stone marks Doc Holliday's grave; according to the inscription, he died in bed.

In the same cemetery—on the pauper's side—under a stone inscribed "Harvey Logan liked Kid Curry," lies a bank robber who once belonged to Butch Cassidy's Hole-in-the-Wall Gang. *FYI:* catch the trail at 12th St. and Palmer Ave., Glenwood Springs.

In the hills surrounding **Black Hawk** and **Central City**, more than ten graveyards—including Masonic, Oddfellows, and Knights of Columbus—became the last resting place of miners and their families. *FYI:* City Hall; 303-582-5251.

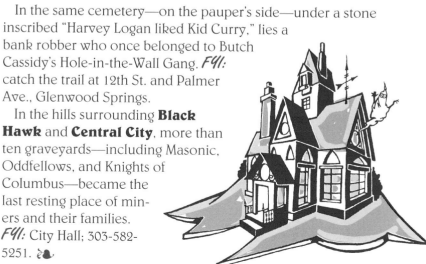

Buffalo Bill's Big Sleep

Colo. Historical Society

Colorado won out over Nebraska and Wyoming as the final resting place of William F. Cody a.k.a. "Buffalo Bill." Cody was most famous for his Wild West Show that toured Europe in the 1880s, but he also had a varied career as a pony express rider, cavalry scout, and buffalo hunter (he was named for the many he killed). He died at the home of his sister in Denver, but he was buried on top of Lookout Mountain. To discourage grave robbers, the grave was topped with concrete and steel bars, but the whole thing had to be taken apart later to fit in Mrs. Cody's coffin. *FYI:* I-70 about 15 miles west of Denver, Exit 256 up Lookout Mountain Rd.; 303-526-0747.

Mysterious Lights

It was a dark and stormy night—well, at least it was dark—in 1882, and a quartet of inebriated miners saw eerie bluish lights above the gravestones of the **Silver Cliff Cemetery**. So many folks have seen the lights since then, *National Geographic* magazine featured the phenomenon. *FYI:* south of Silver Cliff on Hwy. 96.

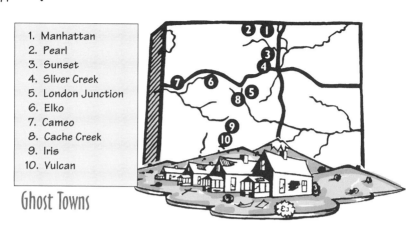

1. Manhattan
2. Pearl
3. Sunset
4. Sliver Creek
5. London Junction
6. Elko
7. Cameo
8. Cache Creek
9. Iris
10. Vulcan

Ghost Towns

Ghosties

Colorado's ghosts are a spooky bunch, but an extra-spiritual encounter needn't be perceived as deadly news. Instead, it might be taken as a ghostly warning to reconsider your actions and reform your errant ways. One thing to keep in mind: considering Colorado's abundance of ghost towns, Victorian homes, and cemeteries, is it any surprise when you bump into the ghostliest of folks?

Ghost and Grave Trivia Quiz

1) Ouray Springs is the site of the great Ute Chief Ouray's last home, where he lived with his wife, _____ or White Singing Bird. She is buried on the property now occupied by the Ute Indian Museum. *FYI:* 303-249-3098.

a) Chipeta **b)** Carol **c)** Birdy

2) The ghost of scout John Fagan (he was buried alive) rides on _____, last seen at Fort Lupton and Bent's Fort.

a) a buffalo **b)** muleback **c)** horseback

3) Espinosa's ghost, _____ body astride a black horse, was last seen in the Sangre de Cristos Pass area.

a) an armless **b**) a headless **c)** a witless

4) The ghost of Edward Bainbridge—who was hung for coveting and killing for _____—was last seen in Georgetown.

a) diamonds **b)** gold **c)** oysters

5) A hideous one-armed ___ was last seen in Leadville's Chippewa No. Six mine.

a) ghost **b)** corpse **c)** chimpanzee

ANSWERS: 1) a 2) c 3) b 4) c 5) a

Getting High

The **Monarch Aerial Tramway** offers riders a legal, if seasonal, high. The observation tower sits on the Continental Divide and the views will take your breath away if the ride up doesn't. *FYI:* near the summit of Monarch Pass, Upper Arkansas Valley; 719-539-4789.

The **Aerial Tramway** in Estes Park will carry you to the 8,896-foot summit of Prospect Mountain. Once atop, you can shop for souvenirs or grab a bite at the snack bar. Open spring through fall. *FYI:* Riverside Dr., Estes Park; 303-586-3675.

Getting Down

Owner Al Mosch leads many of the tours at the **Phoenix Mine** at Idaho Springs, and he tells a story with zest. *FYI:* 303-277-0129.

The very touristy **Lost Gold Mine** in Central City is complete with a singing ore cart. You can walk 220 feet into the old shaft and equipment is on display. This mine produced more than $50 million in gold. *FYI:* 303-582-5913.

The **Bachelor-Syracuse Mine Tour**, Ouray, was featured in *National Geographic* magazine and it's one of the state's best. You'll travel 3,350 feet into the hardrock mine that was named for the three bachelors who worked it in 1884. A real miner guides the tour. Bring your own coat to stay warm. *FYI:* 303-325-4500.

COLORADO FESTIVALS

Gary Nichols

World Championship Pack Burro Race in Fairplay

Party Time!

Small town festivals are a tradition in Colorado. The Western fun usually includes something for the entire family—anything from burro and llama races to draft and driving horse contests.

Bayou Salado Rendezvous, World Championship Pack Burro Race, and World Dry Panning Championship: The burro race has been an annual event since 1949, but this newer and fancier fest is spread out over two weekends (usually in late July). Weekend one includes the Park County Fair and Digger Days mining competitions (plus "whining contest"). These involve a gymkhana, draft and driving horse show, working dog exhibition, and back seat driving contest. Weekend two is the time for the rendezvous, burro and llama races, and panning championships. Period costumes, black powder shooting, tomahawk and knife throwing competitions are all part of the rendezvous. The men's burro race covers 28 miles to an altitude of more than 14,000 feet. Competitors can do almost anything except ride their burros. The women's race is 15 miles. *FYI:* Fairplay; 719-634-4155, ext. 203.

Boom Days: Entertainment, eats, mine-drilling competition, and 26-mile pack burro race to more than 13,000 foot elevation. *FYI:* Leadville, early August; 719-486-3900.

Burro Days: Pack burro races to the top of Mosquito Pass and back to Fairplay. A world championship is at stake, and the iron will of four- and two-footed contestants is inspiring. *FYI:* Fairplay; 719-634-4155, ext. 203.

A mine-drilling competition is part of Leadville's Boom Days

Donkey Derby Days: This has been an annual June event since 1934. Donkeys are ridden six miles over mountain terrain from Victor to Cripple Creek. There's also a kid's race, greasepole climb, and treasure hunt. *FYI:* Cripple Creek; 719-689-2169.

Denver March PowWow: Native American musicians and dancers representing almost seventy tribes from more than twenty states join together for this annual March event. Arts and crafts on are sale. *FYI:* Denver; 303-892-1112.

Pioneer Days: This autumn fest commemorates the discovery of Florence, Colorado, by pioneers. A parade and an arts and crafts fair are part of the festivities. *FYI:* Florence; 719-784-3544.

Hardrockers Holidays: Mining events, horseshoe tourney, wheelbarrow race, and tug-o'-war are all part of this annual summer event. Children's events include Junior Handmucking, a sack race, a frisbee toss, and a three-legged race. If you want to learn more about Double Jacking and Rail Standing, this is for you. Dance. *FYI:* Silverton; 800-752-4494 or 303-387-5654.

San Luis Valley Mountain Men Rendezvous: Buckskin togs, coonskin caps, and muzzle loaders are part of the trappings each August in Del Norte. Competitions including muzzle-loading and tomahawk tossing to the accompaniment of fiddle music. *FYI:* Del Norte; 719-657-2845.

But Wait, There's More . . .

Town Festivals

Leadville's Annual Boom Days: This includes mining competitions, races, parades, and music. *FYI:* Leadville; 719-486-3900.

Leadville's Old Fashioned Fourth of July Celebration: There's a parade, of course, as well as historic tours, an ice cream social, relay races, and fireworks. *FYI:* Leadville; 719-486-3900.

Mountain Man Rendezvous: Each summer enjoy a bit of rough fun that includes ax throwing, black powder matches, buckskin jackets, and a trader's row. *FYI:* Fairplay; 719-481-4249.

Western Arts, Film, and Cowboy Poetry Gathering: Each October, cowboys share their poetry and their art. There are also historical lectures and demonstrations. *FYI:* Durango; 303-247-0312.

All-American Red, White, and Blue Celebration: Enjoy a parade, an all-American hot dog and apple pie picnic, a frog jumping contest, and a street dance. This is also where many Pearl Harbor survivors gather. *FYI:* Grand Lake; 303-627-3402.

Music in the Air

Some of Colorado's town festivals center around music and performing arts. Boulder is famous for its **Colorado Shakespeare Festival**—it ranks among the top three Shakespearean festival in the nation. It is held on the campus of the University of Colorado. *FYI:* Boulder; 303-442-1044.

Folklife Festival: Anglo, Native American, and Hispanic folk traditions and arts and crafts are celebrated each July. There's music and dancing, too. *FYI:* Buena Vista; 719-395-6612.

Great Rocky Mountain Brass Band Festival: Brass bands play pre-1920s music each August. *FYI:* Silverton; 303-387-5654.

Jazz in the Sangres: Each August, this two-day festival is held in the town park under a great tent. A dozen acts will keep your toes tapping, and there's a dance on Saturday night. *FYI:* Westcliffe; 719-783-9163.

Larkspur Renaissance Festival: This annual festival is a concoction of food, theater, crafts, jousting, and merriment in the spirit and tradition of the Renaissance. *FYI:* Larkspur; 303-688-6010.

Leadville Music Festival: Chamber music, dixieland, and opera performed by the best university musicians each July through August. *FYI:* Leadville; 719-486-3900.

Oktoberfest: Each September, Denver's Larimer Square is transformed and you might think you're wandering the streets of Munich. Music, beer, dancing, and general carousing. *FYI:* Denver; 303-892-1112.

Pueblo Chamber of Commerce

The State Fair and Parade are held in Pueblo each year

Scottish-Irish Highland Festival: Each September, this weekend festival includes traditional Celtic sporting events—hammer and tree trunk tossing, for instance—as well as drum major, bagpipe, and sheepdog competitions. *FYI:* Estes Park; 303-586-4431.

Silverton Jubilee Folk Festival: Each June, local and nationally known musicians perform bluegrass, folk, and various other types of musical. *FYI:* Silverton; 303-387-5654.

The **Annual Fat Tuesday Celebration:** This Mardi Gras of the West celebration includes costumes, music, and lot's of food. *FYI:* Breckenridge; 303-453-6018.

Oddballs

And then there are those events and festivals that are theme-oriented or simply don't fit into any niche.

Annual Bear Dance: Each May, this three-day fest celebrates spring. Dancing, singing, traditional ceremonies, and a buffalo feast are all part of the fun. *FYI:* Ignacio; 303-563-9494.

Annual Las Animas Silly Homemade River Raft Race: Unbelievable and truly weird crafts attempt to float and navigate the Arkansas River each July. It's a real question if anyone will reach the finish line. *FYI:* Las Animas; 719-456-0453.

Annual Potato Days: A parade, a raffle, entertainment, barbecued beef, and potatoes are part of this festival in October. *FYI:* Carbondale; 303-963-2733.

Annual Steamboat Cowboy Roundup Days/Fourth of July Celebration: It's a truly Western festival featuring a parade, fireworks, four PRCA rodeos, wild horse and chuck wagon races, and a flapjack feed. Oh yes, and a Rocky Mountain oyster fry. *FYI:* Steamboat Springs; 800-332-3204 or 303-879-0880.

Annual University of Colorado Invitational Mascot Ski Race: Almost fifty college mascots don skis to race downhill each April. *FYI:* Winter Park; 303-726-4118.

Catch the Glow: Puppeteers, carolers, and live window mannequins do their thing during this unusual November celebration. You can also catch the evening parade and enjoy the lights and music. *FYI:* Estes Park; 303-584-4431 or 800-44-ESTES.

Chevrolet Pikes Peak Auto Hill Climb: This is the second oldest auto race in the country, and each July drivers race up a 12.5 mile gravel and dirt course to the summit. Manitou Springs; *FYI:* 719-685-5089.

FibArk Boat Races: The oldest and most prestigious downriver kayak race in the nation. It's a June fest. *FYI:* Salida; 719-539-2068.

Hands Across the Nation: Since 1944, each summer when the Trail Ridge Road reopens, this festival celebrates the link between Estes Park and Grand Lake. *FYI:* Estes Park; 303-584-4431 or 800-44-ESTES.

Heeney Tick Festival: This annual small mountain town party commemorates the recovery of a longtime Heeny resident who survived a tick bite. Each June, you too can get "tick fever" and party your way to health. Food booths and live music. *FYI:* Heeney; 303-668-5800.

St. Patrick's Day Parade: This is the second largest St. Patty's Day parade in the world. It runs five hours and includes 5,000 horses and a varied assortment of humans. *FYI:* Denver; 303-892-1112.

Star Fest and Star Con: These biannual SF conventions are produced by Starland Co. in April and September. Science fiction writers and editors, movie studio publicists, media guests, and fans (including Trekkies) attend. *FYI:* Denver; 303-671-8735.

Strawberry Days Festival: Each June, this celebration includes a rodeo, strawberries, and dancing, as well as an arts and crafts fair. It's the state's oldest civic celebration and it lasts one week. *FYI:* Glenwood Springs; 303-945-6589 or 800-221-0098.

The Mile High Conference: This is Denver's famous science fiction conference for print media. *FYI:* Denver; 303-892-1112.

Wild Mushroom Telluride: Stalk the wild mushroom each August. Experts are on hand to teach you how to identify the poisonous varieties. You can also learn how to grow your own. *FYI:* Telluride; 303-728-3041.

Tumbleweed Festival: On the third weekend in July, this fest includes sidewalk sales, street games, a marathon, softball tournament, golf tournament, and dance. *FYI:* Cheyenne Wells; 719-767-5865.

Watermelon Day: Each August you can indulge in the juicy red stuff that arrives by the truckful. There's also a carnival and parade. *FYI:* Rocky Ford; 719-254-7483.

KIDS' ADVENTURES

Steve Eller

The Colorado State Fair is a favorite for kids of all ages

Fine arts, creative arts, theater, and dance are all part of the **Sangre de Cristo Arts and Conference Center**. Kids will love the hands-on children's museum. *FYI:* Pueblo; 719-543-0130.

Mt. Shavano Trout Hatchery and Rearing Unit: This mega-hatchery has more than a million fish—rainbow, brown, and cutthroat trout, arctic grayling, and kokanee salmon—for kids to count. Millions of fish are hatched each year and then released into the state's myriad streams, lakes, and rivers. *FYI:* Hwy. 291, half-mile northwest of Salida.

Kit Carson County Carousel: Known as "The Jewel of America," this merry-go-round dates to 1905 and is now fully restored; it boasts original paint. Forty-five figures rotate to the accompaniment of the Wurlitzer Monster Military Band Organ. There's only one other carousel of this size and vintage in existence today. *FYI:* 15th St. and Lincoln Ave., Burlington; 719-348-5562.

**Pro Rodeo Hall of Fame and Museum of the American
Cowboy:** American rodeo heroes and heroines are commemorated.
There are multimedia shows, Hall of Champions trophies, belt buckles,
gear, and more. Outdoors, kids will find a mini rodeo arena and
retired rodeo animals. *FYI:* Colorado Springs; 719-593-8847.

Colorado State Fair: Ever since 1872, folks in Colorado have been
celebrating each August. Events include stock shows, rock and country music entertainment, a rodeo, refreshments, and rides. The fun
goes on for ten days. (Reserve motel/hotel accommodations in
advance.) *FYI:* Pueblo, the corner of Prairie and Arroya avenues; 719-
561-8484 or, for tickets only, 800-444-FAIR.

Movie Manor is the
place to stay if you're a
maniac when it comes to
drive-ins. Yes, you can
view the giant screen
from between the sheets.
George Kelloff is the master of ceremonies here—
the Kelloff family started
the tradition in the 1950s
when the kids watched
the drive-in from their
bedroom window. Movie
Manor has been featured
in a PBS special because

it's . . . special. Today, all motel rooms (this is a Best Western) face the
back of the drive-in parking lot and built-in ceiling speakers provide
sound. *FYI:* 2830 W. Hwy 160, Monte Vista; 800-528-1234 or 719-852-
5921.

Folklore and Folklife
At the **Folklife Festival**, mid-July, kids of all ages can view arts and
crafts inspired by Native American, Hispanic, and Anglo folk traditions. Mountain, fiddle, and western-style music and dancing are all
part of the celebration. *FYI:* Buena Vista; 719-395-6612.

Snow sledding in Silverton? Try "Catholic Hill" on 10th Street or 11th
Street next to the Baptist Church. Parents must be on hand at all times
to watch for vehicular traffic.

With 25 wilderness areas, Colorado offers kids many chances to discover nature

Mind Your Wilderness Manners

☞ Stay on trails. Wherever you stray, you kill vegetation and cause erosion.

☞ Camp 100 feet from trails, lakes, and streams.

☞ Use existing campsites whenever possible.

☞ Use gas stoves. Firewood is increasingly scarce, and fire danger is ever-present.

☞ Use biodegradable soap and wash at least 100 feet from water source.

☞ Carry a shovel and bury human waste at least 6 inches below ground.

☞ Pack out all trash!

☞ Leave pets at home; they endanger wildlife and themselves.

☞ Take only pictures and leave only footprints!

River Floats: River running and floating should be attempted only when skilled guides and adults are on hand. Once you've solved that problem, try the Upper Arkansas River for a variety of thrills. A local outfitter will know which areas to avoid. *FYI:* area recreation office; 719-539-7289.

You can enjoy the river from the bank, too

Rockhounding: Ruby Mountain and Mount Antero—both located in the Upper Arkansas River area—are two famous locations for rock hounds. On Ruby Mountain, you may discover spessartite garnets, obsidian pellets, and yellow topaz. Mount Antero—the highest gem field in the U.S.—sparkles with aquamarine and bright blue beryl crystals. Take a rock hound expert with you. *FYI:* Buena Vista Chamber of Commerce; 719-395-6612.

Dinosaur Trivia Quiz

1) Paleontologist Earl Douglass wrote in his diary about finding eight _____ in exact position.

   a) Allosaurus leg bones **b)** Stegosaurus skull bones
   c) Brontosaurus tail bones

2) Fossils of more than seventy dinosaur species were found at the Morrison Formation, including the largest _____ ever excavated.

   a) Apatosaurus
   b) Tyrannosaurus
   c) Pterodactyl

ANSWERS: 1) c 2) a

That's Entertainment!

☛ Traditional Native American dances are performed by tribes at the Manitou Cliff Dwelling. *FYI:* Manitou Springs; 800-642-2567.

☛ Catch a summer repertory of classics and comedy at the Grand Lake Theatre Association. *FYI:* Grand Lake.

☛ Salida's **Powerhouse Players** perform melodramas, mysteries, and comedies in the town's historic steam plant building. *FYI:* Salida; 719-539-2455.

☛ For more than 25 years, the **Greeley Chorale** has been serenading area audiences. *FYI:* Greeley; 303-356-5000.

INDEX

Other Books from John Muir Publications

Asia Through the Back Door, 4th ed., 400 pp. $16.95 (available 7/93)

Belize: A Natural Destination, 336 pp. $16.95

Costa Rica: A Natural Destination, 2nd ed., 310 pp. $16.95

Elderhostels: The Students' Choice, 2nd ed., 304 pp. $15.95

Environmental Vacations: Volunteer Projects to Save the Planet, 2nd ed., 248 pp. $16.95

Europe 101: History & Art for the Traveler, 4th ed., 350 pp. $15.95

Europe Through the Back Door, 11th ed., 432 pp. $17.95

Europe Through the Back Door Phrase Book: French, 160 pp. $4.95

Europe Through the Back Door Phrase Book: German, 160 pp. $4.95

Europe Through the Back Door Phrase Book: Italian, 168 pp. $4.95

Europe Through the Back Door Phrase Book: Spanish & Portuguese, 288 pp. $4.95

A Foreign Visitor's Guide to America, 224 pp. $12.95

Great Cities of Eastern Europe, 256 pp. $16.95

Guatemala: A Natural Destination, 336 pp. $16.95

Indian America: A Traveler's Companion, 4th ed., 448 pp. $17.95 (available 7/93)

Interior Furnishings Southwest, 256 pp. $19.95

Mona Winks: Self-Guided Tours of Europe's Top Museums, 2nd ed., 448 pp. $16.95

Opera! The Guide to Western Europe's Great Houses, 296 pp. $18.95

Paintbrushes and Pistols: How the Taos Artists Sold the West, 288 pp. $17.95

The People's Guide to Mexico, 9th ed., 608 pp. $18.95

Ranch Vacations: The Complete Guide to Guest and Resort, Fly-Fishing, and Cross-Country Skiing Ranches, 2nd ed., 396 pp. $18.95

The Shopper's Guide to Art and Crafts in the Hawaiian Islands, 272 pp. $13.95

The Shopper's Guide to Mexico, 224 pp. $9.95

Understanding Europeans, 272 pp. $14.95

Undiscovered Islands of the Caribbean, 3rd ed., 288 pp. $14.95

Undiscovered Islands of the Mediterranean, 2nd ed., 224 pp. $13.95

Undiscovered Islands of the U.S. and Canadian West Coast, 288 pp. $12.95

Unique Colorado, 112 pp. $10.95 (available 6/93)

Unique Florida, 112 pp. $10.95 (available 7/93)

Unique New Mexico, 112 pp. $10.95 (available 6/93)

A Viewer's Guide to Art: A Glossary of Gods, People, and Creatures, 144 pp. $10.95

The Visitor's Guide to the Birds of the Eastern National Parks: United States and Canada, 410 pp. $15.95

2 to 22 Days Series

Each title offers 22 flexible daily itineraries useful for planning vacations of any length. Aside from valuable general information, included are "must see" attractions *and* hidden "jewels."

2 to 22 Days in the American Southwest, 1993 ed., 176 pp. $10.95

2 to 22 Days in Asia, 1993 ed., 176 pp. $9.95

2 to 22 Days in Australia, 1993 ed., 192 pp. $9.95

2 to 22 Days in California, 1993 ed., 192 pp. $9.95

2 to 22 Days in Europe, 1993 ed., 288 pp. $13.95

2 to 22 Days in Florida, 1993 ed., 192 pp. $10.95

2 to 22 Days in France, 1993 ed., 192 pp. $10.95

2 to 22 Days in Germany, Austria, & Switzerland, 1993 ed., 224 pp. $10.95

2 to 22 Days in Great Britain, 1993 ed., 192 pp. $10.95

2 to 22 Days Around the Great Lakes, 1993 ed., 192 pp. $10.95

2 to 22 Days in Hawaii, 1993 ed., 192 pp. $9.95

2 to 22 Days in Italy, 208 pp. $10.95

2 to 22 Days in New England, 1993 ed., 192 pp. $10.95

2 to 22 Days in New Zealand, 1993 ed., 192 pp. $9.95

2 to 22 Days in Norway, Sweden, & Denmark, 1993 ed., 192 pp. $10.95

2 to 22 Days in the Pacific Northwest, 1993 ed., 192 pp. $10.95

2 to 22 Days in the Rockies, 1993 ed., 192 pp. $10.95

2 to 22 Days in Spain & Portugal, 192 pp. $10.95

2 to 22 Days in Texas, 1993 ed., 192 pp. $9.95

2 to 22 Days in Thailand, 1993 ed., 180 pp. $9.95

22 Days (or More) Around the World, 1993 ed., 264 pp. $12.95

Automotive Titles
How to Keep Your VW Alive, 15th ed.,
464 pp. $21.95
How to Keep Your Subaru Alive
480 pp. $21.95
How to Keep Your Toyota Pickup Alive
392 pp. $21.95
How to Keep Your Datsun/Nissan Alive
544 pp. $21.95
**The Greaseless Guide to Car Care
Confidence,** 224 pp. $14.95
Off-Road Emergency Repair & Survival, 160 pp. $9.95

TITLES FOR YOUNG READERS AGES 8 AND UP

"Kidding Around" Travel Guides for Young Readers
All the "Kidding Around" Travel guides are 64 pages and $9.95 paper, except for **Kidding Around Spain** and **Kidding Around the National Parks of the Southwest**, which are 108 pages and $12.95 paper.
Kidding Around Atlanta
Kidding Around Boston,2nd ed.
Kidding Around Chicago, 2nd ed.
Kidding Around the Hawaiian Islands
Kidding Around London
Kidding Around Los Angeles
Kidding Around the National Parks of the Southwest
Kidding Around New York City, 2nd ed.
Kidding Around Paris
Kidding Around Philadelphia
Kidding Around San Diego
Kidding Around San Francisco
Kidding Around Santa Fe
Kidding Around Seattle
Kidding Around Spain
Kidding Around Washington, D.C., 2nd ed.

"Extremely Weird" Series for Young Readers. Written by Sarah Lovett, each is 48 pages and $9.95 paper.
Extremely Weird Bats
Extremely Weird Birds
Extremely Weird Endangered Species
Extremely Weird Fishes
Extremely Weird Frogs
Extremely Weird Insects
Extremely Weird Mammals (available 8/93)
Extremely Weird Micro Monsters (available 8/93)
Extremely Weird Primates
Extremely Weird Reptiles
Extremely Weird Sea Creatures
Extremely Weird Snakes (available 8/93)
Extremely Weird Spiders

"Masters of Motion" Series for Young Readers. Each title is 48 pages and $9.95 paper.
How to Drive an Indy Race Car
How to Fly a 747
How to Fly the Space Shuttle

"X-ray Vision" Series for Young Readers. Each title is 48 pages and $9.95 paper.
Looking Inside Cartoon Animation
Looking Inside Sports Aerodynamics
Looking Inside the Brain
Looking Inside Sunken Treasure
Looking Inside Telescopes and the Night Sky

Multicultural Titles for Young Readers
Native Artists of North America, 48 pp. $14.95 hardcover
The Indian Way: Learning to Communicate with Mother Earth, 114 pp. $9.95
The Kids' Environment Book: What's Awry and Why, 192 pp. $13.95
Kids Explore America's African-American Heritage, 112 pp. $8.95
Kids Explore America's Hispanic Heritage, 112 pp. $7.95

Environmental Titles for Young Readers
Rads, Ergs, and Cheeseburgers: The Kids' Guide to Energy and the Environment, 108 pp. $12.95
Habitats: Where the Wild Things Live, 48 pp. $9.95
The Kids' Environment Book: What's Awry and Why, 192 pp. $13.95

Ordering Information
Please check your local bookstore for our books, or call 1-800-888-7504 to order direct from us. All orders are shipped via UPS; see chart below to calculate your shipping charge to U.S. destinations. **No P.O. Boxes please; we must have a street address to ensure delivery.** If the book you request is not available, we will hold your check until we can ship it. Foreign orders will be shipped surface rate unless otherwise requested; please enclose $3.00 for the first item and $1.00 for each additional item.

For U.S. Orders Totaling	Add
Up to $15.00	$4.25
$15.01 to $45.00	$5.25
$45.01 to $75.00	$6.25
$75.01 or more	$7.25

Methods of Payment
Check, money order, American Express, MasterCard, or Visa. We cannot be responsible for cash sent through the mail. For credit card orders, include your card number, expiration date, and your signature, or call (800) 888-7504. American Express card orders can be shipped only to billing address of cardholder. Sorry, no C.O.D.'s. Residents of sunny New Mexico, add 6.125% tax to total.

Address all orders and inquiries to:
John Muir Publications
P.O. Box 613
Santa Fe, NM 87504
(505) 982-4078
(800) 888-7504